BRIDGEND LIBRARY AND INFORMATION SERVICE

3 8030 01572 0223

Just World

A FABIAN MANIFESTO

Fabian Globalisation Group

Zed Books
LONDON & NEW YORK

in association with

The Fabian Society

BRIDGEND LIBRARY & INFORMATION SERVICE	
Bertrams	08.08.05
320.01	£12.99
1111/05	

Just World was first published in 2005 by
Zed Books Ltd, 7 Cynthia Street, London N1 9JF, UK and
Room 400, 175 Fifth Avenue, New York, NY 10010, USA
www.zedbooks.co.uk

in association with
The Fabian Society, 11 Dartmouth Street, London SW1H 9BN
www.fabian-society.org.uk

Copyright © The Fabian Society 2005

The rights of the Fabian Society to be identified as the author of this work have been asserted by it in accordance with the Copyright, Designs and Patents Act, 1988

Cover designed by Andrew Corbett
Typeset in 10/13 pt Palatino
by Long House, Cumbria, UK
Printed and bound in Malta
by Gutenberg Press Ltd

Distributed in the USA exclusively by Palgrave Macmillan, a division of
St Martin's Press, LLC,175 Fifth Avenue, New York, NY 10010

All rights reserved

A catalogue record for this book
is available from the British Library

US Cataloging-in-Publication Data
is available from the Library of Congress

ISBN Hb 1 84277 454 9
Pb 1 84277 455 7

This book, like all publications of the Fabian Society, represents not the collective views of the Society but only the views of the authors. This publication may not be reproduced without express permission of the Fabian Society.

Contents

Abbreviations	vii
Acknowledgements	ix
Notes on Contributors	x

Part 1 • Social Democracy and Globalisation   1
ADAM LENT

1. Introduction   3
2. Social Democracy and the Global   6
3. The Crisis of Globalisation   16

Part 2 • A New Global Economic Settlement   33

4. Regulating and Improving Global Financial Flows   35
   STEPHANY GRIFFITH-JONES AND RICARDO GOTTSCHALK
5. Allocating a Global Levy   46
   BOB DEACON
6. A New Global Monetary Architecture   52
   JAMES B. QUILLIGAN

Part 3 • Building Global Democracy and Peace   63

7. Rethinking Democracy for a Global Age   65
   DAVID HELD
8. Rethinking Peace, Security and Human Rights for a Global Age   73
   MARTIN SHAW

Part 4 • Creating Equitable Trade   79

9. Equitable Trade and Development   81
   ALAN HUDSON

Part 5 • Improving Global Regulation and Governance   101

10   Employment Regulation in a Global Economy   103
     JOHN EVANS
11   Protecting the Environment through Global Regulation   114
     CRAIG BENNETT
12   An Equitable Approach to Migration   125
     RUSSELL KING AND MARK THOMSON

Part 6 • The Politics of Global Change   133
     ADAM LENT

13   Building a Movement for Global Change   135
14   Conclusion: The Four Pillars of Progressive Global Change   141

Notes   146
Index   153

Abbreviations

ACP	African, Caribbean and Pacific (countries)
ASEAN	Association of South East Asian Nations
ATC	Agreement on Textiles and Clothing
CAP	Common Agricultural Policy
CBI	Confederation of British Industry
CCL	Contingency Credit Line
CCM	Country Coordinating Mechanism
CFF	Compensatory Financing Facility
CSD	UN Commission on Sustainable Development
CSR	corporate social responsibility
ECA	export credit agency
ECOSOC	Economic and Social Committee
EEC	European Economic Community
EIA	environmental impact assessment
EPZ	export-processing zone
EU	European Union
FOEI	Friends of the Earth International
GATT	General Agreement on Tariffs and Trade
G20	Group of Twenty (larger developing countries)
G33	Group of Thirty-three (agricultural developing countries)
G7	Group of Seven (wealthiest countries)
G8	Group of Eight (wealthiest countries)
G90	Group of Ninety (poorest developing countries)
GDP	Gross domestic product
Gea	global economic account
GETO	Global Environment and Trade Organisation
GIN	global issues network
GM	genetically modified
GPPN	global public policy network
GRI	Global Reporting Initiative
GUF	global union federation
ICFTU	International Confederation of Free Trade Unions
ICTY	International Criminal Tribunal (Yugoslavia)

IFI	international financial institution
IFF	International Finance Facility
IGO	intergovernmental organisation
ILO	International Labour Organisation
IMF	International Monetary Fund
KPI	key performance indicator
LDC	less-developed country
Mercosur	Comisión Sectorial para el Mercado Común del Sur (Southern Common Market)
MFA	Multifibre Arrangements
NATO	North Atlantic Treaty Organisation
NCP	National Contact Point
NGO	non-govermental organisation
OECD	Organisation for Economic Cooperation and Development
PPP	Purchasing Power Parity
PRGF	Poverty Reduction and Growth Facility
PRSP	Poverty Reduction Strategy Paper/Process
SAARC	South Asian Association for Regional Cooperation
SADC	Southern African Development Community
SDR	Special Drawing Right
SDT	special and differential treatment
SRI	socially responsible investment
TNC	transnational corporation
TRIPs	Trade-Related Intellectual Property Rights
TUAC	Trade Union Advisory Committee
UK	United Kingdom
UN	United Nations
UNCTAD	United Nations Conference on Trade and Development
UNDP	United Nations Development Programme
UNESCO	United Nations Educational, Social and Cultural Organisation
UNRISD	United Nations Research Institute for Social Development
USA	United States of America
WDM	World Development Movement
WHO	World Health Organisation
WTO	World Trade Organisation
WWF	World Wildlife Fund

Acknowledgements

This book is one of the outcomes of the Fabian Society's project on globalisation launched in 2002. Thanks go to the many people who have taken part in that project in whatever capacity and, of course, to those who have contributed to this volume. This includes Craig MacDonald and others who helped with the research for the book.

The project as a whole owes a particular debt to Michael Jacobs and Adrian Harvey, former General Secretary and Deputy General Secretary of the Fabian Society, who commissioned and supported the project with great enthusiasm and ability.

The patience and work of Robert Molteno and the other staff at Zed is also greatly appreciated.

Adam Lent

Notes on Contributors

Craig Bennett is Senior Campaigner on Corporate Accountability at Friends of the Earth.

Bob Deacon is Professor of International Social Policy at the University of Sheffield.

John Evans is General Secretary of the Trade Union Advisory Committee of the Organisation for Economic Co-operation and Development.

Ricardo Gottschalk is a Fellow in the Institute of Development Studies at the University of Sussex.

Stephany Griffith-Jones is Professorial Fellow in the Institute of Development Studies at the University of Sussex.

David Held is Graham Wallas Professor of Political Science at the London School of Economics.

Alan Hudson is Committee Specialist for the International Development Select Committee of the United Kingdom House of Commons. He writes here in a personal capacity.

Russell King is Professor and Co-Director of the Sussex Centre for Migration Research at the University of Sussex.

Adam Lent is an independent Research and Policy Consultant and co-ordinator of the Fabian Society project on globalisation.

James B. Quilligan is Director of the Brandt 21 Forum.

Martin Shaw is Professor of International Relations and Politics at the University of Sussex.

Mark Thomson is Research Officer in the Sussex Centre for Migration Research at the University of Sussex.

Part 1
Social Democracy and Globalisation

ADAM LENT

1
Introduction

What would a just world look like? Such a question is hardly fashionable today amongst our ultra-pragmatic politicians and cynical journalists. But it is a question we cannot avoid, not only because the just seem so hard-pressed by those who dream of self-interested domination but also because the world – the global – is the new locus of the struggle for real change.

In this book, a clear vision of a just world is proposed. Fundamentally, it is one based on four pillars that oppose the thrust of the ideology of global change that has dominated the last forty years. These pillars are: the creation of a new global economic architecture to enable expansionary national economic policies; democratic global governance; equitable trade; and regulation of corporate and governmental action in the global sphere.

The ways in which each of these pillars can be built are open to very detailed debate, to which the ideas presented below are a contribution. Yet the pillars are braced by a single common feature. They are about introducing a permanence and solidity into the global arrangements for justice that currently only exists meaningfully in the drive to liberalise markets and defend corporate interest.

Binding treaties and powerful institutions armed with dire sanctions now straddle the world to ensure the marketisation of much of the global economy. Yet nothing of any equivalence exists to drive out poverty, improve educational standards, defend nascent welfare programmes, or ensure that companies do not abuse their workers. Such matters are left to the mercy of the chaotic global monetary system, are based on voluntary and non-binding agreements, or are pursued by bodies with unreliable sources of income and no hard power.

A commitment to this greater solidity and permanence means that, amongst other things, this book calls for a formally allocated global levy instead of aid; an ordered global monetary system designed to encourage growth and stability rather than the chaos that increases indebtedness and uncertainty; legal regulation of corporate activity rather than the voluntary pacts of corporate social responsibility; and the requirement of democracy and respect for human rights as a condition for national membership of global bodies.

But the conundrum at the heart of this book is that the force that might most effectively build permanence and solidity for the value of global justice is profoundly weak. That force is the 'progressive Left' political strand within the wealthy Northern economies, but today the Left's once-powerful social base – an active and economically dominant industrial working class – has disappeared, and the progressive vision is in a permanent process of adapting to the global economic reality created by the New Right and its corporate allies since the 1960s. What remains of the movement seems split three ways between those leading that adaptation, those who have retreated into the pursuit of nothing more than the material interests of trade union members, and those who cling valiantly to the vision of a progressive political shift led by their respective nation states, as though the global changes of the last forty years had never happened.

This situation will ensure that the fundamental principles of the progressive Left will continue to have no serious impact on the global stage – and hence on its own domestic contexts – when it is squeezed by the sharpening conflict between the three forces mentioned above. Current notions that these values can have a global impact when aligned with a united and more forceful European Union can invoke only a wry smile. Why should the EU leaders pursue such a policy? In global trade negotiations, where such values might really count, the EU has hardly covered itself in progressive glory. Without coordinated and significant pressure from below, political leaders will always opt for the path of least resistance – in this case, national economic self-interest dressed up as neoliberal idealism.

This book argues that, despite this gloomy prognosis, the progressive Left can again become a genuine force for global good if it meets some key challenges. The Northern version of the global justice movement should not be romanticised. It undoubtedly has a powerful grassroots energy on occasion but it is divided by institutional rivalries, lacks any sustained vision of global change, and has no grounding in any social or economic base. Its appeal is almost entirely moralistic and it has no concept of building a global justice movement in the North that struggles for Northern rather than Southern interests.

By contrast, any genuinely effective movement for global change based in the North must develop an agenda and vision that benefits Northern populations and tackles the same neoliberal forces that afflict the South. In all likelihood, this agenda will be based on the loss of workplace rights over the last thirty years and the rise of an uncontrolled consumerism that has brought with it a wide range of unwanted consequences, from the death of the high street to the targeting of children by aggressive marketing techniques. These are the two most noticeable effects in the North of the increasing freedoms granted to corporations since the 1960s. Most importantly, they are concerns that could speak directly to the service sector class that is now the most significant economic group in the world's advanced economies.

In addition, a progressive campaign for change cannot be focused primarily on the nation state as agent of change, with the global seen as an afterthought. A national government may present itself as the bearer of significant policy change but, in truth, it is one player in a complex global network of competition, negotiation and compromise involving many other players – other states, regional governments, corporations, global institutions and others. While no progressive movement for change can ignore the nation state, primarily such a movement must insert itself as a player in this global game, drawing its legitimacy from grassroots support and its power from an ability to disrupt economies by mobilising that support. At heart, this means pressurising the corporations, regional governments and other global institutions ranged alongside the state.

While these imperatives cannot be met either easily or speedily, that should not be reason to avoid them. Somewhere between the 1970s and 1990s, the progressive Left was cowed and lost the capacity to think big. Remaining world-weary and prudent may have become the most comfortable position for the Left. But in an age when there are plenty of people thinking very big for the Right and for the religious fundamentalists, this defensive position is fraught with risk, not just for the Left but for the world itself.

2
Social Democracy and the Global

Social democracy is an approach committed to finding a balance of economic interests between different groups in society through democratic processes of negotiation. However, historically a great flaw has limited the capacity of social democracy to sustain itself in Western Europe and to expand to less developed economies: while social democrats have been relatively successful at ensuring a balance of economic interests at a national level within Western Europe, they have been far less successful at creating structures and cultures to achieve a similar balance at a global level. This chapter will show that while such a balance appeared to have been found between 1945 and the late 1960s, it was only as the result of contingent and temporary factors. Once these altered, national and corporate economic self-interest was allowed to flourish without check. The result has been a global economic and political environment much more hostile to the maintenance of social democratic policies in Western Europe and their expansion elsewhere.

What is Social Democracy?

Social democracy originally emerged within the socialist movement of the early twentieth century as an alternative to revolutionary socialism. Its proponents believed that the transfer to a socialist society had to be achieved through democratic and peaceful means, either because revolution was no longer possible or because it was undesirable.

However, as social democrats successfully entered mainstream politics and government in Western Europe after 1945, gradually and increasingly the vision of a socialist society has been replaced by a more pragmatic approach. Accepting that capitalism does bring great benefits – particularly economic growth and innovation – this approach nevertheless emphasises that state intervention is required to ameliorate the problems of capitalism – particularly material inequality, worker exploitation, poverty and economic instability.

In government, social democrats employed a toolkit of policies to achieve their goal of humanising and stabilising capitalism. These have included state ownership of and investment in key sectors of the economy, some protection of the domestic economy from foreign competition and interests, a major expansion of social security payments, regulation of business practice (particularly in the field of employment and trade union rights) and the provision or facilitation of free healthcare, free social services, free education and cheap housing. The major expansion of state activity and spending that this required was funded largely through a significant increase in taxation of various forms, government borrowing and post-war economic growth.

Following the economic problems of the 1970s, the influence of New Right thinking in the 1980s and increasing globalisation (see below), some of these policies are less favoured by social democrats than they once were. State ownership, state investment, protectionism and very high levels of taxation and borrowing have all fallen out of favour with most social democrats, to be replaced by a more classical approach to economic control. However, a strong commitment to free, quality public services, cheap and decent public housing, and significant social security provision funded by a sustainable tax base remains almost universal amongst social democrats.

Social Democracy's National Successes

Within the nations of Western Europe, the historical record of social democracy is undoubtedly mixed. The grander vision of a truly classless society in which poverty, significant inequality of wealth and social division have been eliminated remains unattained, although some would argue that the Scandinavian nations have come close. In addition, the hope that significant state control and investment in national economies would end economic instability and recession were ill-founded. However, as is explored below, this may have as much to do with the social democratic failure to influence the principles and policies governing the global economy as with any inherent failure in social democratic policies themselves.

However, if the era after 1945 is compared to the period prior to 1939, it is clear that social democratic policies and principles have proved remarkably effective. Levels of poverty and inequality have been very significantly reduced across Western Europe, while social mobility has increased. Perhaps more importantly, access to free education, free healthcare, cheap housing and decent social security payments has ensured that the consequences of being on a low income or being unemployed are not the personal or family disaster they once were.

As a direct result of social democratic and progressive policies in the post-war period, Western Europe is immeasurably better educated, healthier and fairer than it was before 1939.

Social Democracy's Global Failures

At the global level, the influence of social democratic principles and policies has been far weaker than at the national level within Western Europe. This has meant not only that levels of global inequality, poverty and instability are still unsustainably high, but also that key international factors enabling social democratic progress in Europe after 1945 were gradually eroded at the end of the late 1960s, setting back the progressive cause for many years. To understand this, it is necessary to outline a narrative of global economic development that is widely overlooked within popular and intellectual political debate.[1]

Across the political spectrum there is scant awareness that much of the shift to and then away from social democratic policies in Western Europe and elsewhere was in large part determined by the nature of the global economic settlement that developed during and after the Second World War.

Three interlinked elements of the post-war settlement were particularly central to the success of social democracy in Western Europe. The first was *the provision of very significant amounts of American cash to enable Western Europe to rebuild its shattered economies after 1945*. Without this money, social democrats could never have delivered on their promises to reconstruct national economies after the war, let alone creating a fairer society based on significant public spending, state investment and wealth redistribution. This period of 'dollar reconstruction' lasted at least until 1951.

Second, *sustained economic growth across Western Europe from 1951 to the late 1960s allowed social democratic policies to gain long-term credibility*, form the new consensus and build a tax base, while governments maintained their creditworthiness with lenders. This growth was in very considerable part made possible by the willingness of American governments to ensure global financial stability by pegging the dollar to the price of gold and to allow the dollar to be used as the currency of international trade and exchange.

Third, *the same period of economic growth in Western Europe was made possible by protectionist policies* – such as tariffs, subsidies and exchange controls – that allowed infant or reviving domestic industries to grow and reinvest with little foreign competition. Such protectionism was very much against the principles to which the American government had committed itself and Britain in the two years after the war, when global free trade was seen as best for America and for the world as a whole. Indeed, given America's bankrolling of international economic growth, the limitations placed on trade and investment opportunities by European governments were particularly resented in Washington.

However, American administrations were willing to rein in their attempts to impose a wider free trade settlement for two key reasons. First, they were aware that political stability in Western Europe required policies that could guarantee full employment and social justice and thus weaken the appeal of extremist politics, particularly communism. Second, American governments did not want to alienate Western European nations, particularly West Germany, as they hoped to contain the influence of the Soviet Union during the Cold War.

This availability of the dollar and tolerance of protection allowed social democratic governments to embark on ambitious programmes for full employment and social justice. They also protected such governments from having to undertake deflationary policies such as public spending cuts and raised interest rates, which had been the common reaction to national trade and government deficits in the decades before 1939, and which had made the pursuit of costly progressive policies so problematic.

However, there was strong awareness amongst progressive European governments that their reliance on a global economic system based upon the continued willingness of American governments to ensure financial stability and tolerate protectionism was perilous. A change in economic conditions, American government or the global geopolitical situation could easily lead to a shift in policy in Washington. Indeed this is what happened from 1968 onwards, but in the meantime a series of proposals by leading social democrats had been aiming to establish a global economic system that would assure national governments of funds for investment in times of weak growth, recession or indebtedness, and protect such nations from fluctuations in international finance.

The most famous of these was the International Clearing Union proposed by John Maynard Keynes at the Bretton Woods negotiations to develop post-war international economic institutions held in 1944. Keynes's vision was to establish an international trading currency, independent of any single national economy and easily accessible by governments requiring investment funds, within institutional rules that would require nations to avoid both trade surplus and deficit, thus introducing great stability into international finance. Keynes's proposal was rejected by American negotiators, and even the compromise agreed at Bretton Woods was almost entirely dissolved in further negotiations over the next three years.

Similar, if less ambitious, proposals appeared at regular intervals, particularly when the system went through its periodic crises. These included a programme proposed by the British Chancellor, Stafford Cripps, in 1949; the Prebisch Report of the early 1960s; the Algiers Charter in 1967; and even a proposal from President de Gaulle in the same year. The last three were notable for the fact that they devised settlements to fund and protect progressive policies not only in Europe but also in the developing world, which was increasingly making its presence felt in international diplomacy and the global economy. However, all of these proposals went the same way as Keynes's – ultimately defeated by American opposition.

Events were soon to bear out the fears of those proposing these alternative global arrangements. During the 1970s the global economic settlement that had existed since the mid-1940s broke down, creating huge pressure on national governments to adopt the deflationary policies feared by social democrats. The reasons for this collapse were complex but three key factors can be identified.

The first element was *the decision of the Nixon administration to end the link between the dollar and gold in 1971*. As the dollar was widely regarded as overvalued, this was, in effect, a devaluation. As is often the case with devaluations, the decision was taken primarily to allow the American economy to regain its competitiveness without Nixon having to take painful steps such as cutting public spending or raising interest rates. Despite attempts to establish a new international monetary system, this decision created a global economy based on floating exchange rates, with vast amounts of uncontrolled capital available and large trade surpluses and deficits between nations – factors that could only encourage inflation and instability.

The second element was *the rise in the price of oil*, in part engineered by the Organisation of Petroleum Exporting Countries (OPEC) and in part caused by instability in the Middle East during 1973–4 and 1979–81. This caused a very significant rise in prices across the developed world, making inflation and the state response to it the prime policy concern of the period, as opposed to the key goals of full employment and social justice that had dominated the post-war period up to that date.

The third element was *the growth of 'footloose capital' in the 1960s*. As a result of the introduction of greater currency convertibility at the end of the 1950s and the rise of the new multinational corporations searching for the best return on their vast cash reserves, the ability of national governments to control the flow of money in and out of their economies weakened. This was significant because it gave business both the power and the incentive to oppose the usual methods progressive governments employed to control inflation: incomes policies, price controls and restrictions on the size of bank deposits. These methods became increasingly unpopular with business as they limited the new-found freedom of capital, while that freedom itself became feared by governments, worried that their policies might drive investment out of their economies. As a result, traditional deflationary policies – cutting spending, raising interest rates – made a widespread comeback, despite their inevitable social costs.

As inflation and the pressure for deflationary policy increased during the 1970s in the wake of the collapse of the post-war global economic settlement, progressive governments and parties did not simply sit back and accept their fate. As in the 1940s–60s, a series of proposals was advanced to establish an ordered system that would be more friendly to national progressive policies. This time, however, the proposals took on an ever-greater sense of urgency as national governments increasingly found themselves having to cut spending and raise interest rates, resulting inevitably in higher levels of unemployment.

These proposals included the Barber Plan of 1971 and the Volcker Plan of 1972, which bore some similarities to a Keynesian approach and had support amongst US officials shocked by Nixon's unilateral action on the dollar. The New International Economic Order, which developed out of the Algiers Charter and was proposed by the United Nations, gained increasing attention and support from the developing world throughout the 1970s. This emphasised a global economic system that would prioritise economic growth in the South by reordering relations between the developed and developing world. This spirit also informed other programmes such as those developed by the Conference on International Economic Cooperation and the Lomé Convention, which did actually change some of the conditions for trade between the European Economic Community (EEC) and 46 developing world countries. The best-known proposal, however, was the Brandt Report, which created much debate and attracted widespread attention for its comprehensive plans to stabilise the world economy – along Keynesian lines – while encouraging economic growth in the developing world.

However, all of these proposals finally fell foul of disunity within and between progressive governments in the developed and developing worlds and the growing influence of neoliberalism and monetarism, which offered explanations and solutions for the problem of inflation and had no time for schemes of global cooperation designed to make the world safe for expansionary policies. Conveniently, of course, the neoliberal perspective also suited big business, which increasingly saw the crisis of the 1970s, coupled with the polemics of Friedman and von Hayek, as a way to win the freedom to increase profits.

During the 1980s the election in the developed world of political leaders committed to deflationary policies as a matter of principle and keen to remove restrictions on the freedom of business to transfer capital, goods and production processes across borders ensured that the old system of progressive policies was laid to rest for good. In its place was a far more chaotic and competitive global economic arrangement that increasingly required governments to cut spending and raise interest rates in times of economic difficulty or in the face of external shocks, and to enact business-friendly policies, particularly with regard to labour market flexibility, in order to ensure investment capital did not trickle out of their domestic economies.

The 1980s also saw a forthright attempt to challenge progressive policies in the developing world. Southern countries that found themselves in economic difficulties and in urgent need of funds or new financial arrangements to limit the damage done by spiralling government debt or trade deficits were required by bodies such as the International Monetary Fund (IMF) and the World Bank to undertake just the sort of deflationary and market liberalisation policies that were being pursued in the developed world. In this way, financial speculators and multinational corporations were able to gain significant involvement and freedom of action in the economies of the developing as well as the developed world.

The collapse of communist governments across Eastern Europe from 1989 removed the final obstacle to the extraordinary worldwide spread of the ideology of neoliberalism and its corporate partners, who inevitably followed in the wake of its implementation. This, coupled with the rapid rise of Internet technology and new financial techniques, particularly derivatives, consolidated the freedom of business to invest, trade and produce where it wished, leading to the now common claim that we live in a new era of economic globalisation.

Three Options for Social Democracy in the Age of Globalisation

The crisis this global shift has created for social democracy has been profound and long-lasting. Since the late 1970s, social democratic parties have found themselves facing an international economic environment that is increasingly hostile to their historical approach to domestic economic policy. Where once there was an effective if flawed system of international cooperation designed to fund and protect progressive domestic policies, we now have a largely unregulated approach dominated by competition between nations for corporate investment. In this climate, the economic pressure is intense to overturn or avoid progressive policies – higher taxes, trade union rights, business regulation – that offend corporate decision makers. Social democrats, progressives and those they represent have paid a high price for their failure to reform the global economy in as rigorous a fashion as they reformed the post-war national economies of Western Europe.

Under these conditions, social democrats face three options. The first is to ignore the changed global economic environment and simply press for domestic policies associated with the post-war era – an approach urged by left-wing traditionalists across European social democratic parties and labour movements. The almost certain result of this would be to lose international investment and face economic disaster and hence further failure for the social democratic project.

The second is to accept the domestic imperatives of the new global economic environment but pursue social democratic objectives as much as possible within the new constraints. This is the approach taken in its most thoroughgoing way by Tony Blair in the United Kingdom, although it has influenced social democrats around the globe to a considerable extent. The main negative consequence of this is that the freedom of manoeuvre for social democrats to pursue genuinely progressive policies in any permanent form can be very restricted. Blair's project has been helped by a decade's worth of economic growth and stability. Should the UK face an economic downturn, there is little doubt that the Labour government would be under very great pressure to raise interest rates and cut spending in just the same way as its predecessor in the 1970s. Under those conditions many of the financially costly progressive policies pursued by Blair would be either undone or, at least, halted.

The third option is to develop and campaign for a global order that would allow once again the wholesale pursuit of progressive policies. This book attempts to sketch the outline of just such a global order. However, it looks very different to that pursued after 1944. There is no attempt to allow one nation's goodwill and self-interest to determine the success of the system and there is certainly no attempt to allow one nation's self-interest to rule in one sphere of action – economic, military or political – in return for restraint in another. These were the flaws that led, after 1944, to the collapse of the 1970s. The vision proposed here is about creating a system in which a balance of economic interests is created and maintained through peaceful, democratic negotiation – the very principle that underlay domestic social democratic reform in Western Europe.

To that end the approach is based on four pillars adapted from the history of social democracy for the new era of globalisation. These are:

- a new global economic architecture to enable expansionary national economic policies;
- democratic global governance;
- equitable trade;
- regulation of corporate and governmental action in the global sphere.

The details of these foundational policies are provided in Part Two.

This, of course, raises important questions about why this vision should ever see the light of day as concrete policy. The post-1944 settlement only occurred in the first place because it suited the contemporary interests of the USA. This matter is dealt with in Part Three.

3
The Crisis of Globalisation

The Global Governance System

In theory, the system of global governance is based upon a series of multilateral institutions established by international treaties in the years following the end of the Second World War. While each of these institutions has a set of specific goals enshrined in its founding treaty, they are all supposed to govern on the basis of free negotiation, impartial settlement of disputes and the spirit of international cooperation. In reality, each of these institutions has been designed or manipulated to work overwhelmingly in the interests of the world's dominant national powers. In addition, as the last chapter showed, when the interests of these powers diverge, the USA has managed to ensure that its interests gain priority. More will be said about this below, but first we provide brief details of the most significant institutions of global governance.

The United Nations (UN): Established in 1945, the UN is primarily charged with preventing the outbreak of military conflict by promoting peaceful settlement of disputes and acting against those threatening world peace. Over time the responsibilities of the UN and its agencies have expanded to include a wide range of concerns such as the promotion of economic and social development, protection of the environment, defence and promotion of human rights, emergency relief and protection of refugees. Its main governing bodies are the General Assembly, the Secretariat and, most notably, the Security Council.

The World Trade Organisation (WTO): The WTO was only established in 1993. However, it represented the creation of a permanent institutional form for the ongoing negotiations or 'rounds' of the General Agreement on Tariffs and Trade (GATT), which began in 1948. The WTO's stated mission is to make trade flow smoothly and freely, and to make the rules governing trade transparent, fair and predictable. To this end its main roles are to implement trade agreements, act as a forum for trade negotiations, and make judgements in trade disputes. The governing body of the WTO is the Ministerial Council.

The International Monetary Fund (IMF): Established in 1944, the IMF's main goal is to maintain stability in the international financial system. It has done this chiefly by lending funds to nations suffering serious balance of payments difficulties. It is also charged with preventing fluctuations in the currency exchange markets and competitive currency devaluations by national governments. Its governing body is the Board of Governors.

The World Bank: The International Bank for Reconstruction and Development was founded in 1944. Along with some smaller associated institutions, it is known as the World Bank. The Bank's prime aim is to provide funds to help finance economic development within developing and poor countries. Its governing body is the Board of Governors.

Group of Eight (G8): The Group of Eight is an annual meeting designed to coordinate the international policies of the eight richest nations and to influence the policies of the institutions of global governance. The first G8 summit was held in 1975.

The Organisation for Economic Cooperation and Development (OECD): Founded in 1962, the OECD acts largely as a body facilitating and supporting policy development for the industrialised economies. However, it has also negotiated legally binding agreements, largely in the area of finance.

Alongside these institutions of global governance, there are also a series of regional institutions designed to promote economic, political, legal and/or military cooperation amongst neighbouring countries: these include the North Atlantic Treaty Organisation (NATO), the EU, the Association of South East Asian Nations (ASEAN), Mercosur, and OPEC.

Although each of these institutions is in theory designed to promote international cooperation and peace, there are three main ways in which the world's dominant powers have ensured that the system of global governance works to promote their interests.

The Structural Bias in Global Governance

Most of these key institutions of global governance have in-built biases in favour of the world's dominant national powers. The United Nations General Assembly may be based on a 'one nation, one vote' principle, but the UN constitution offers permanent membership and the power of veto in the far more influential and powerful Security Council only to the USA, the UK, France, China and Russia. Voting strengths on the Board of Governors of both the World Bank and the IMF are allocated in proportion to financial contribution to the organisation's coffers, in effect giving greater formal power to the richest nations. The G8 is a highly elitist body, restricted by definition to the eight wealthiest nations. The OECD may have a broader membership, but is still only open currently to thirty wealthy countries.

The only organisation which has a governing body genuinely based on a 'one nation, one vote' principle is the World Trade Organisation. However, here the world's leading nations have sought to undermine the political equality built into the structure through extensive use of caucus-style meetings to which only a select few are allowed entry, threats and promises regarding political and economic sanctions and favours to buy votes, and overwhelming dominance in terms of research and lobbying capacity to win arguments and persuade key supporters (see box opposite).

Five ways in which the WTO process is distorted to serve the interests of the advanced economies

1 *Bullying*. In *Behind the Scenes at the WTO* (2003), Jawara and Kwa conclude that negotiations at the WTO are conducted in a climate of fear. Focusing on the Doha Agreement, they accuse the USA and the EU of being the worst offenders. Operating a divide-and-rule strategy, they are able to dangle the carrots of financial aid, technical assistance, bilateral and multilateral debt relief and preferential trade agreements in front of developing countries too desperate to refuse. Crucially, such moves aim to pre-empt alliances by other countries to challenge this power differential.

2 *Standards protectionism*. Larger economies effectively ban imports from the least developed countries (LDCs) on the grounds that the standard of the product is too low. Possible health risks are advanced to endorse this policy. Oxfam (2002: 103) cites the case of the EU imposing a ban on African exports of nuts, dried fruits and cereal on the grounds that they may contain dangerously high levels of the naturally occurring carcinogen aflatoxin. Even though the policy doesn't create significant health benefits, it is estimated to cost African exporters US$670 million per year. LDCs often lack both the technical expertise to comply with these standards and the means to contest adverse decisions.

3 *Dominating negotiations*. While this may not be an explicit strategy of the larger economies, it is a natural outcome of their financial advantage, which allows them to station more negotiators at the WTO in Geneva. The World Development Movement (WDM) points out that 30 of the 134 countries simply can't afford to locate negotiators in Geneva (www.wdm.org).

4 *Enforcement of disputes*. The framework of the WTO makes enforcement of judgements more difficult for LDCs. The dispute panel is responsible only for the arbitration. Responsibility for enforcement lies with the individual country favoured in the ruling. Thus, in the case of a decision in favour of an LDC against a major economy, the

latter will have little to fear from trade sanctions. The reverse situation, however, clearly does not apply.

5. *Subsidies*. Despite the commitment to reduce agricultural subsidies, larger economies have continued to operate the same policies by deploying what Oxfam calls a 'game of semantics' (2002: 113). By redefining subsidy into the 'blue box' and 'green box' categories, the US and EU have continued to provide support to their own agricultural sectors, which affects decisions about production and also the price at which the goods can be exported to other countries. Indeed, the so-called 'emergency payment' to US farmers to cover weather damage is now distributed as a matter of course. According to an Oxfam briefing paper, the US government is more willing to listen to 25,000 cotton farmers than to the WTO. Despite WTO rulings against most of its cotton subsidies, the USA seems determined to continue with its policies, possibly endangering the next round of talks, to protect a small share of its export market, Oxfam (2004: 6).

Sources

Fatoumata Jawara and Aileen Kwa (2003) *Behind the Scenes at the WTO : the Real World of International Trade Negotiations*, London and New York: Zed Books, in association with Focus on the Global South (Bangkok).

Oxfam (2002) *Rigged Rules and Double Standards: Trade, Globalisation and the Fight against Poverty*, available to download at www.oxfam.org.uk

Oxfam (2004) *One Minute to Midnight: Will WTO Negotiations in July Deliver a Meaningful Agreement?* Briefing Paper 65, available to download at www.oxfam.org.uk

The Ideological Bias in Global Governance

All of the key institutions of global governance, with the arguable exception of the UN and the World Bank, are charged primarily with implementing the principle of global free trade. At one level, this means creating the conditions of economic and political stability that allow international trade to flourish. However, it also means taking practical steps to remove the barriers traditionally erected by national governments to protect their economies from external competition. The main barriers include forbidding foreign companies to invest or trade in all or parts of an economy, imposing tariffs whereby those importing certain goods must pay extra levies, subsidies for domestic companies that make them more competitive on cost, placing restrictions on the inflows and outflows of money, and artificially lowering the value of the domestic currency to make imports more expensive relative to domestically produced goods and services.

Under classical economic theory, which extols the benefits of free trade, the widespread removal of these barriers should allow developing and poorer economies to expand by virtue of their newfound access to foreign investment capital and to foreign markets, particularly in the advanced economies where they would be able to compete on price given their lower labour and production costs. The system should also benefit the advanced economies, which should enjoy access to new markets and sources of labour in the developing and poorer countries, particularly for the sale and production of their more refined goods and services.

However, while a great deal of rhetoric has been produced by the institutions of global governance and the advanced economies on the benefits of free trade, particularly since the 1980s, these same advanced economies have been far more thoroughgoing in their assault on barriers to free trade in the developing and poor world than in their own countries. Thus while the structural bias in key institutions has been used alongside the promise of favours and threats of sanctions to 'liberalise' Southern economies, the use of subsidies, tariffs and other barriers is still widespread in advanced economies to prevent firms from the developing and poor economies gaining equal access to Northern markets (see box, pages 22–28).

Eight examples of discriminatory trade practice by the developed world

1 Common Agricultural Policy (CAP)

The creation of a Common Agricultural Policy was proposed in 1960, became the biggest policy concern of the European Community in its early days, and is still one of the major challenges facing the EU. Although spending on CAP has been reduced in recent years, it still consumes almost half the EU budget and spending will amount to £29.3 billion in 2004.

CAP reforms agreed to on 26 June 2003 are set to change the nature of agricultural support in the EU. The agreement begins to break the link between subsidies and production whilst also creating an explicit link with environmental standards. Over the past decade, the way in which CAP supports farming has been changing. Originally, it relied mostly upon high prices to provide a reasonable income for farmers. These prices were sustained by strict restrictions upon imports and other forms of price manipulation.

The system had two main problems: it encouraged massive overproduction and disrupted international trade. Not only were imports of agricultural produce from developing countries prevented by high duties, but the surplus produce was exported with the help of large subsidies, often with a deflationary effect on international prices, further hindering producers in developing nations attempting to gain some market share in agricultural products. Until the Uruguay Round of trade talks, which started in 1987, world trade negotiations had concentrated upon pressing for freer trade in industrial goods only. The inclusion of the agricultural sector marked what many hoped was the beginning of the end for CAP. However, the six biggest contributors to the EU budget want to see present levels of spending frozen for 2007–13. Three quarters of the world's 1.2 billion poor people live and work in rural areas; agriculture is therefore crucial to their survival and fight against poverty. Nearly 3 billion people – half the world – live on less than $2 a day. This is less than the support received by the average European cow through CAP.

2 *Cotton*

Low prices on world cotton markets are driving millions of people in West and Central Africa deeper into poverty. Typically, the crop is grown on small family farms in Benin, Chad, Mali, Burkina Faso and Togo – some of the poorest countries in the world, where cotton accounts for between 37 and 71 per cent of agricultural export earnings. Prices began to decline in the mid-1990s before reaching an all-time low in October 2001. One of the major reasons behind the slump in prices is overproduction and dumping of exports by the USA, the largest net exporter. While international prices for cotton were at the all-time low, US cotton producers received subsidies totalling $2.3 billion dollars in one season, further encouraging overproduction and export – to the extent that 68 per cent of US cotton produced in 2003 was exported, mostly at prices below the true cost of production. US cotton is produced by 25,000 plantations, the ten largest of which receive annual subsidies totalling approximately $17 million. In the EU, Greek and Spanish producers have benefited from $700 million in annual CAP subsidies. Consequently, a small cotton producer in Mali is lucky to make $400 a year whilst US producers receive $250 per hectare. The direct loss to West Africa as a result of these protectionist measures is estimated to be $250 million a year. The passing of the US Farm Act in 2002 means that these subsidies are likely to continue for some time.

3 *Sugar*

The EU sugar regime is of significance for developing countries. Europe is now the biggest exporter of white sugar to the rest of the world, despite having some of the world's highest costs of production for sugar. It is an unreformed sector of CAP, heavily reliant on export subsidies (sugar represents 30 per cent of the EU's annual export subsidy bill), price support and high levels of dumping. It costs Europe around €673 to produce one tonne of white sugar, compared to just €286 for competitive countries like Brazil, Colombia, Malawi, Guatemala and Zambia. Europe's farmers and processors are the world's biggest recipients of sugar subsidies, and sugar prices are maintained at almost three times world market levels, protected by tariffs that reach 140 per cent, compared to most EU tariffs which are less than 5 per cent. The livelihoods of agricultural labourers and small farmers in developing countries suffer both as a consequence of the EU's exports to world markets, and because of restricted access to European markets. Translated into foreign exchange losses, world market distortions associated with EU sugar policies cost Brazil $494 million, Thailand $151 million, and South Africa and India around $60 million each in 2002. These are large losses for countries with significant populations living in poverty.

4 *Dairy sector*

The EU dairy sector is heavily protected under the CAP through a system of price support, production quotas, import restrictions, and export subsidies. The OECD estimates that in 2001 the EU supported its dairy sector to the tune of €16 billion. Although its world market share has declined in recent years, the EU remains one of the biggest exporters of milk and milk products in the world, accounting for 40 per cent of whole milk powder exports, 32 per cent of cheese exports, 31 per cent of skimmed milk powder exports, and 20 per cent of butter exports. The EU can only maintain its position in world markets because of the export subsidies made available under the CAP dairy regime. In order to enable the export of EU dairy produce, subsidies are provided to bridge the gap between prices on the world market and the higher internal EU prices. Without tariffs, the high internal EU prices for dairy products would attract large volumes of imports. Therefore, the EU maintains high tariffs against imports of dairy produce in order to protect domestic producers from competition. In 2001, EU import tariffs were as high as 150 per cent for butter, more than 50 per cent for skimmed milk powder, and above 60 per cent for whole milk powder. The EU dairy regime affects developing countries in three main ways: by depressing world market prices, by pushing developing country exporters out of third markets, and by directly undermining domestic markets in developing countries. These affect both major developing-country dairy exporters, such as Argentina, and poor countries seeking to develop or maintain their domestic dairy industries, such as the Dominican Republic, India and Jamaica.

5 *Textiles*

The trade in textiles and clothing is important for developing countries and amounts to nearly 6 per cent of world exports. Manufacture of clothing is a labour-intensive activity: the sector is therefore particularly important for the creation of employment opportunities in these economies. For years, the instrument of intervention was the quota system applied on exports from developing countries. A recent study produced jointly by the IMF and the World Bank in September 2002 estimated the export revenue loss to developing countries due to industrial country quotas and tariffs at US$40 billion per year, of which $22.3 billion is on account of quotas. The same study also pointed out that as many as 27 million jobs are forgone in developing countries as a result of quotas and tariffs. These quotas were inherited from the Multifibre Arrangements (MFA) but are now governed by the Agreement on Textiles and Clothing (ATC). After a 10-year period ending on 1 January 2005, the ATC will expire and all quotas will be abolished. So, in 2005, all WTO members are supposed to have unrestricted access to the European, American and Canadian markets.

6 Bananas

The European Union is a very significant player in the world banana trade, importing about a third of all traded bananas – about the same amount as the US, but more than three times as much as the third biggest importer, Japan. More than 85 countries produce bananas and plantains, but for at least 15 Latin American and Caribbean producer countries, the banana is a crucial source of export income. Several million people depend on the banana trade for their livelihood. For the group of African, Caribbean and Pacific (ACP) countries that signed the Lomé Convention, a trade and aid agreement that the EU first signed in 1975 with 48 of Europe's ex-colonies, the Convention's preferential trade arrangements permitted duty-free access for a range of commodities, including bananas, on which the economies of the ACP are extremely dependent. This market access was not extended to the so-called 'dollar banana' exporting countries, which are in Central and South America. In most of the 12 traditional ACP banana-exporting countries, the cost of production was approximately twice as high as for dollar bananas. In the case of European producers – Canary Islands (Spain), Martinique and Guadeloupe (French territory in the West Indies), Madeira and the Azores (Portugal) and Crete (Greece) – the cost could be up to three times as high. Higher production costs meant that these countries and regions could only compete in a protected market. Conscious of this, the EU set up a system of quotas and tariffs (and a system of direct support to its own banana farmers) to limit the entry of dollar bananas. The resulting internal price on the European market, substantially higher than the world price, enabled ACP and European producers to survive on the market. Preferential access to the European market was to protect them from direct competition with dollar bananas.

In 1996, a little more than a year after the establishment of the WTO, five countries – Honduras, Guatemala, Ecuador, Mexico and the United States – lodged a complaint against elements of the European banana regime that they considered to be 'discriminatory' to their interests, claiming they did not have sufficient access to the European market. After a prolonged trade war and threats of sanctions, agreement was finally reached in April 2001. The agreements meant, at least in the short term, the end of the banana wars. A new transitional reformed regime came into force on 1 July 2001, of which the principal measures were: the end of the division of the dollar quota into national allocations, and the transfer of 100,000 tonnes of the ACP quota to the dollar quota. This transitional regime is to be replaced on 1 January 2006 by a tariff-only regime for dollar bananas – with neither quotas nor licences. A tariff-only regime would remove the restrictions on the volumes of bananas imported, but does allow the EU to keep in place the tariff preference for the ACP banana imports, at least until 2008.

7 Rice

Rice is also one of the most distorted cereal commodities on the global market. Both wealthy and poor countries use a variety of methods to control their rice imports and exports. Japan charges an over-quota tariff on the import of grains other than wheat, reaching a ludicrous 1,000 per cent in 2001. The European Union uses export subsidies to promote its own production, and is responsible for 95 per cent of global export subsidies on rice. The United States uses credit guarantees for rice farmers and also sends out a sizeable portion of its export rice crop as food aid. Japan has traditionally been one of the most ardent supporters of agricultural protectionism and price supports. Japan's government resisted rice imports for over 30 years, but, at the conclusion of the Uruguay Round of global trade negotiations in 1995, Japan agreed to a quota on rice. Since 1999, Japan has used a tariff-rate quota system for rice imports, mostly purchased by the government. Within the quota, the tariff is zero. Japan's import quota for rice and rice products is 770,000 tons per year. This represents 7.2 per cent of average consumption. However, most of this rice is not released directly into Japan's market. Instead, imported rice often remains in government stocks until it is released as food aid to developing countries. Tariffs as high as 490 per cent have discouraged exporters from selling beyond the current tariff-free quota for the year. Direct subsidies are also employed, and at the turn of the century amounted to almost $2 billion. The world's largest producers of rice are China, India, Indonesia, Bangladesh, Vietnam, Thailand, Myanmar and the Philippines. Developing countries are the main players in world rice trade, with shares of 83 per cent of total exports and 85 per cent of total imports.

8 *Groundnuts (peanuts)*

Groundnuts are one of the world's main oilseed crops. The crop is widely cultivated in developed and developing countries and provides a livelihood and cash income to many poor farmers in the developing world, especially in sub-Saharan Africa and Asia. In Senegal an estimated one million people (one tenth of the population) are involved in groundnut production and processing. Groundnuts account for about 2 per cent of GDP and 9 per cent of exports. Historically, world groundnut markets have been distorted by heavy government intervention designed to stimulate production through subsidies and price supports, or to protect producers by controlling imports and extending production support, along with liberalisation. Since the mid-1990s, all major exporters have gradually liberalised their groundnut sectors, in part to fulfil their commitments under WTO agreements. Results are mixed, however, and trade in groundnuts remains heavily distorted. The US groundnut policy, highly distorted by large subsidies and prohibitive tariffs between 1930 and 2001, was recently reformed, but with high and redundant tariffs still in place. The 2002 Farm Act eliminated some unsustainable features of previous legislation (high support prices and production quotas) but introduced new distortions that have the potential to depress world market prices and subsidise producers. Prohibitive tariffs of almost 150 per cent remain. Full trade liberalisation would raise market prices by

> about 19 per cent for groundnuts, 18 per cent for meal, and 17 per cent for oil. Although the net world welfare gains of liberalising groundnut markets are moderate, they are still significant for small agrarian economies. Liberalisation of the value-added markets – oil and meal – would result in even larger welfare gains in African countries. The WTO has estimated that African countries such as Gambia, Malawi, Nigeria, Senegal and South Africa would experience aggregate net welfare gains of $72 million, with Senegal and Nigeria gaining most. The increase in world prices after trade liberalisation would lead to a total gain for African groundnut producers of some $124 million in profits. These figures are sizeable for small African economies.

This is a double blow to poorer economies in that it stifles the economic benefits they may accrue from access to richer markets but also allows Northern firms to enter developing country economies and use their advantages (often resulting from government subsidy) to destroy competition.

The neoliberal tag often attached to the policies of institutions of global governance and their wealthiest backers is in fact a misnomer. Neoliberal implies a genuine commitment to the principles of free trade that informed the original liberal thinkers of the nineteenth century. What, in fact, has existed for many years is a system built on the promotion and protection of the interests of the most advanced economies at the expense of the interests of the developing and poor economies.

Evading Institutions of Global Governance

On those rare occasions when the most powerful nations have proved unable to pursue their interests within one or more institutions of global governance, they have simply ignored the processes and decisions of those institutions and operated either within a more compliant institution or outside of the institutional structure of global governance altogether. The most striking and notable example of this has been the 2003 invasion of Iraq, which saw the USA assemble a group of national allies to support its invasion when it proved impossible to win backing at the UN Security Council.

It has to be noted that this evasion of the usual institutional routes for global governance is not always the result of the most powerful nations operating at the expense of weaker nations. It more usually results from the powerful nations failing to agree a course of action amongst themselves. Thus when the UN failed to back military action within Kosovo largely because of Russian objections, the USA and the UK used NATO to mobilise and sanction intervention.

However, in recent years, the evasion of global governance processes has taken on the clear appearance of policy, particularly on the part of the USA. Since George W. Bush came to power in 2000, the goal of US foreign policy has been to consolidate and expand America's position as the sole economic, political and military superpower both at a global level and within all regions of the world. Clearly such a policy could not be pursued within institutions of global governance where other advanced nations possess significant political power. As a result, the Republican administration simply denounced existing treaties and operated outside the bounds of multilateral institutions.

This shift has been particularly clear in the WTO. Historically the USA was a strong backer of the WTO and the GATT negotiations which preceded its establishment. However, in recent years developing countries have acted in a more united fashion and employed the political equality existing in the structures of the WTO to act more effectively in their own interests. This has led to the failure to reach final agreements at both the Seattle and Cancun WTO summits in 1999 and 2003. In addition, developing countries have also won significant cases against the protectionist policies of advanced economies through the WTO dispute resolution process.

Increasingly the response of the US government has been to ignore the WTO and to negotiate bilateral deals on trade with individual nations that suit its own interests better and leave it free to use the traditional methods of threat and favour that used to work at the WTO.

The Resulting Crisis

The persistent use of these three strategies has ensured that the most powerful nations have successfully pursued their own economic, political and military interests through the system of global governance since 1945. The result has been predictable. Western Europe, the USA and Australasia have enjoyed a much greater period of economic growth and political stability in comparison to the rest of the world. Only in Japan and South East Asia has there been comparable economic growth, although this has been achieved largely by resisting the liberalisation agenda of the United States until the 1990s. Nevertheless, this region clearly has nothing close to the global political and military influence of America. The more recent, and very mixed, economic success of China and India has also been achieved with protectionist policies and some gradual liberalisation.

However, those areas of the developing world that have been brought most completely within the political, military and economic sphere of America and Western Europe – Latin America, the Caribbean, Africa and, more recently, Eastern Europe – have proved far less able to pursue their own interests and have endured lesser growth and stability as a result. For example, on a number of measures levels of inequality are now serious, growing and highly unsustainable (see box, pages 31–2).

Five measures of growing global inequality

1 Human Development Index (HDI)

The Human Development Index was defined by the 2004 *Human Development Report* as a three-fold measure combining measures of life expectancy, school enrolment, literacy and income to give a broad view of a country's development. Twenty countries have seen a decline in their HDI over the course of the 1990s, an unprecedented development. Of the 20 countries, 13 are in sub-Saharan Africa.

The top five countries and the values they achieved on this index are as follows:
1 Norway (0.956)
2 Sweden (0.946)
3 Australia (0.946)
4 Canada (0.943)
5 Netherlands (0.942)

The bottom five are:
173 Burundi (0.339)
174 Mali (0.326)
175 Burkina Faso (0.302)
176 Niger (0.292)
177 Sierra Leone (0.273)

2 The probability at birth of surviving to the age of 65

For those living in sub-Saharan Africa the probability is:
36 per cent for women
32 per cent for men

For those people living in an OECD country:
88 per cent for women
79 per cent for men

3 *Life expectancy at birth*

Sub-Saharan Africa:
  1970–5 estimate
  45.2 years

  2000–5 estimate
  46.1 years

OECD countries:
  1970–5 estimate
  70.4 years

  2000–5
  77.2 years

4 *Infant mortality rate (per 1,000 live births)*

For those children born in sub-Saharan Africa in 1970 infant mortality stood at 139, while for children born in an OECD country this figure was a much lower 40.

For those children born in sub-Saharan Africa in 1992 infant mortality stood at 108, while for children born in an OECD country this figure was 11.

5 GDP *per capita* (PPP US$)
- OECD countries $24,904
- Sub-Saharan Africa $1,790
- South Asia $2,658
- Latin America and the Caribbean $7,223
- East Asia and the Pacific $4,768
- Arab states $5,069

(All data sourced from UNDP, *Human Development Report 2004*.)

The possible destructive outcome of this ongoing crisis has been detailed in the Introduction. The Introduction outlined four ways in which an alternative global model based upon a genuine balance of interests can be developed. The next part now explores these four pillars in much closer detail.

Part 2
A New Global Economic Settlement

4
Regulating and Improving Global Financial Flows[2]

STEPHANY GRIFFITH-JONES AND
RICARDO GOTTSCHALK

The universally accepted Monterrey Consensus identifies both domestic and foreign private investment as vital financing sources for growth and development. However, despite low-income countries' efforts to promote private investment through policy improvements and economic-institutional reforms, levels of private finance are still largely insufficient to meet their development financing needs. As a consequence, official development assistance (ODA) remains a crucial source of finance for the majority of low-income countries. The failure by developed countries to meet the financing commitments undertaken at Monterrey in 2002, seen as necessary for the achievement of the Millennium Development Goals, is a source of concern.

This chapter has as its primary objective to indicate ways through which development finance to low-income countries could be significantly increased. First, it provides recent estimates of external financing needs for sub-Saharan Africa, a developing region where most low-income countries are located. The majority of low-income countries face a significant gap between resources available and resources required to meet the Millennium Development Goals. Second, the chapter discusses new and current proposals for a substantial increase in development finance: in our view these proposals deserve strong support, and action from progressive governments in the developed countries. The proposals include the International Finance Facility put forward by the UK Treasury and public mechanisms to encourage private flows, especially to support infrastructure investment. In addition, we discuss new official financing facilities to help developing countries deal with external shocks, particularly terms-of-trade shocks. Finally, the chapter presents a proposal for amplifying the developing country voice in the international financial institutions (IFIs). The proposal also addresses concerns raised by the Monterrey Consensus, on the need to make IFIs more participatory, transparent and democratically accountable.

Low-income Countries' Financing Needs

Low-income countries clearly need external finance in support of growth and development. In what follows, we provide estimates of how much external finance the sub-Saharan African region, where most low-income countries are located, needs to meet the millennium poverty-reducing target by 2015.

To estimate such needs, we used a savings gap model.[3] The projected external financing needs for sub-Saharan Africa and for all other developing regions are provided in Table 4.1.

Table 4.1 Net External Financing Needs of Developing Countries, by Regions

	Annual average poverty reduction target scenario* 2004–15	
	US$ billion[†]	% GDP
East Asia & Pacific	n.d.	n.d
South Asia	36.9	3.4
Middle East & North Africa	67.5	6.5
Sub-Saharan Africa	61.9	10.8
Europe & Central Asia	n.d.	n.d
Latin America & the Caribbean	188.7	5.9

Source: R. Gottschalk (2004) 'How much external finance will be needed to meet the poverty-reducing target by 2015?' paper prepared as part of the Comprehensive Evaluation of the African Development Fund 1996–2000.
L. Hanmer, N.D. Jong, R. Kurian and J. Mooij (1999) 'Are the DAC targets achievable? Poverty and human development in the year 2015', *Journal of International Development*, 11, no. 4, pp. 547–63.

Notes: * Growth rates used in the poverty reduction target scenario are drawn from Hanmer *et al.* (1999), also reported in DFID (1999).
† The values are set in 2002 constant prices.

As can be seen from Table 4.1, to meet the poverty-reducing target set by the international community, sub-Saharan African countries (all of which are low-income members) need external finance amounting to US$62 billion on average per year between now and 2015, far more than they are currently receiving. Our projected external financing needs are not too dissimilar to, but clearly higher than, those obtained by the UN Millennium Project, of about US$42 billion.[4]

According to recent estimates by the World Bank (see Global Development Finance 2004), total net private capital flows to developing countries reached US$208 billion in 2003. Sub-Saharan Africa received only US$12.4 billion, or just 6 per cent of the total. This figure confirms concerns that low-income countries have very restricted access to private sources of external finance. It is equally important to notice that such sources fall far short of the total external financing required by sub-Saharan Africa to meet the millennium poverty-reducing goal by 2015. This gap should therefore be filled with aid flows. However, current aid flows are clearly insufficient to fill this gap.

To illustrate the point, three main developing regions of the world – the Middle East and North Africa, South Asia, and sub-Saharan Africa – received only a total of US$26.6 billion of net private flows in 2003 (which shows that total net private flows to developing countries are still geographically highly concentrated), whereas their projected total external financing needs to meet the poverty reduction target for 2015 are US$166 billion a year (see Table 4.1). The remaining external financing gap of

Table 4.2 Net Private Capital Flows and Net External Financing Needs (US$ billion)

	Net private capital flows in 2003	External financing needs (poverty reduction target scenario) 2004–15	Remaining external financing gap (to be filled with aid flows)
South Asia	10.4	36.9	26.5
Middle East & North Africa	3.8	67.5	63.7
Sub-Saharan Africa	12.4	61.9	49.5
Total	26.6	166.3	139.7

Source: World Bank (2004) *Global Development Finance 2004* and Table 4.1.

these three developing regions is therefore nearly US$140 billion, which should be filled with official flows (see Table 4.2). However, even if all the aid flows to developing countries in 2002 – US$58 billion – went just to these three developing regions, the remaining financing gap would still be over US$80 billion.

The message from the above is clear: aid flows to developing countries must be at least doubled until 2015 if the Millennium Development Goals are to be achieved. At the same time, long-term private flows should be encouraged.

Public Mechanisms for Increasing Capital Flows to Developing Countries

This section discusses mechanisms through which development finance to support growth and development can be enhanced. First, to increase aid flows to developing countries, we will discuss the International Finance Facility (IFF) proposed by the UK Treasury; if implemented, this facility could increase significantly the current level of aid flows through raising private resources in the international capital markets. Second, to encourage private capital flows, especially to infrastructure projects, we will discuss proposals for new guarantee mechanisms. Third, to help developing countries deal with external shocks that are outside their control, we discuss proposals for improving IMF lending facilities.

The International Finance Facility

This sub-section discusses the proposal by the UK Treasury on creating an IFF, aimed at doubling the current levels of aid flows to developing countries until 2015.

To double the current levels of aid flows, the IFF proposes to frontload aid flows by raising private resources in the international financial markets through issuing bonds. The operation would be secured by commitments from donors to provide multi-year streams of annual payments to the IFF.[5]

The disbursements of resources raised would be concentrated in the years up to 2015, while the streams of donors' income to the IFF would be distributed over a 30-year period. Not all donors would have to agree to the facility: provided a few donors support it, it can be implemented.

The levels of income commitment would be decided by each donor, and would be subject to 'high-level' financing conditions; these, if not met by the recipient countries, would permit donors to suspend their payments. However, to reduce bondholders' uncertainties and thereby ensure that the bonds issued by the facility achieve the highest possible rating, a number of rules would be imposed.

1 The conditions the recipient country would have to meet would be very general – not becoming subject to UN sanctions, for example;

2 No country would be permitted to receive more than 5 per cent of total disbursements, thereby diluting the possible impact of one country breaching the conditions on donors' income payments; and

3 The IFF would be limited to raising capital to the equivalent of 85 per cent of the net present value of its future income.

At the same time, donors would have to follow a set of principles in their disbursement programmes. These would probably include requirements that the resources be untied, used for poverty alleviation, provided on a multi-year basis, disbursed mainly in the form of grants, and concentrated in low-income countries (UK Treasury and DFID 2003: 6).

The proposed facility and the conditions attached to it are fully consistent with the international consensus reached at Monterrey on the need to increase aid flows substantially in the years up to 2015, and to use these flows to help the poorer countries to achieve the international development targets. It seems important to emphasise that the IFF should be seen as a complement to, and not a substitute for, directly increasing aid.

The proposed facility is thus a very important mechanism in support of development finance. A key feature is its flexibility – in the levels of resources donors would have to commit to it, in how resources can be disbursed, and in the number of committed donors required to launch it. The initiative has the support of a number of developing countries. However, among the industrialised relatively few have offered clear support to the initiative so far. It is therefore important that the powerful momentum to support the initiative is created in 2005, when the UK holds the EU presidency and hosts the G8 Summit.

Guarantees for private flows, especially for investment in infrastructure

Finance needs for the establishment of infrastructure in developing countries are large. According to the UN Millennium Project, they amount to US$10 per person across sub-Saharan Africa. There is therefore an urgent need to attract private investors to infrastructure projects.

Public guarantees can clearly play this role. Existing public guarantee mechanisms (granted by the Multilateral Development Banks and Export Credit Agencies) play a positive role in mitigating risks of long-term investment and loans to fund important activities such as infrastructure development.[6]

Existing guarantees have positive features in that they increase flows and extend maturities of debt instruments in developing countries. According to the World Bank, the total available is up to twelve times what it would have been without guarantees. Another positive feature of guarantees is their ability to reduce spreads. Loan guarantees may also affect the interest rate pertaining to the non-guaranteed private credits.

A first policy proposal is for lifting existing ceilings for heavily indebted poor countries (HIPCs) to borrow. A key problem for low-income countries, especially HIPCs, is how to attract sufficient private medium- or long-term lending. There are at present two sets of constraints on low-income countries attempting medium-term borrowing from banks (bonds would seem to be even more difficult). The first set of constraints relates to official institutions. In particular, under the terms of many Poverty Reduction and Growth Facilities (PRGFs), the government and public sector of HIPCs are restricted to zero non-concessional borrowing. This is mainly a by-product of the conditions set for HIPC debt relief, and to a certain extent is linked to the fact that this debt relief may have been somewhat insufficient. However, the HIPC Initiative should ideally do for low-income countries what the 1989 Brady Plan did for countries like Mexico, which was to help acquire or restore access to private credits. For this purpose, one may hope that future agreements with the IMF will allow the HIPC governments and public sectors to have some positive non-concessional borrowing.

A second policy proposal refers to a necessary expansion of public guarantees. As regards medium-term borrowing by the private sector, which is crucial for more rapid growth in low-income countries, the key difficulty is its perceived low creditworthiness.

Official guarantee mechanisms are therefore crucial. Guarantees offered by the World Bank and International Finance Corporation (IFC) need to be expanded. Similarly, export credit agencies (ECAs) should maintain or restore cover when HIPC debt relief is granted. This would help overcome the current contradiction between granting debt relief to help restore creditworthiness and flows, and an unwillingness to restore guarantee cover, which would help companies to have access to such flows.

Therefore, measures to encourage private lending require: (1) international action, including lifting ceilings in IMF programmes to allow the government and public sector to borrow; and (2) action by multilaterals and developed governments to restore export credit cover and/or create new mechanisms – through co-financing, as well as guarantees – that will encourage private lending to the low-income countries' private sector, at levels compatible with debt sustainability.

Finally, a further issue refers to the pro-cyclicality of international private flows. It is widely accepted that international financial and banking markets tend to overestimate risk in difficult times and underestimate it in good times. As a result, private lenders are prone to boom–bust patterns that are often more determined by changing global preferences for risk aversion than by country fundamentals. This provides a strong case for public institutions to play an explicit counter-cyclical role to help compensate for the inherent tendency of private flows to be pro-cyclical.

Improving IMF lending facilities to help developing countries deal with external shocks

An important way of increasing official liquidity in times of external shocks is to expand the counter-cyclical role of the IMF through the creation, expansion or improvement of its facilities for these purposes. For middle-income countries, this could imply, for example, the creation of a more effective 'son/daughter' of the suspended Contingency Credit Line (CCL), that would help prevent or moderate capital-account-led crises.

Such a 'new' CCL could be automatically available to all countries that were very favourably evaluated by the IMF in their Annual Article IV consultations, if they had balance of payment problems arising from international financial contagion. An alternative would be that after a positive evaluation in Article IV consultations, a country would become eligible for a 'new' CCL. The fact that countries would be named as eligible for the 'new' CCL by the IMF would make it a sign of strength (indicator of good policies) rather than a sign of possible future weakness, which the old CCL was perceived to be.

For middle-income countries it could also imply liberalising the very high conditionality linked to the Compensatory Financing Facility (CFF), which can help countries compensate for terms of trade shocks, and thus allows for more growth by reducing the temporary burden of adjustment. The changes required would not only imply modifications of the facilities, but also – where appropriate – reducing and streamlining their conditionality and making it more effective in supporting growth.

As regards low-income countries, one of the most appropriate mechanisms to provide additional IMF funding if the country faced external shocks outside its control could be to increase significantly access under the PRGF arrangements (a measure called PRGF augmentation in recent IMF analysis) and to reduce conditionality as well as making the conditionality more supportive of growth and poverty reduction by, for example, allowing higher levels of government spending, particularly when this implies positive impacts on pro-poor growth.[7]

Given that about half the eligible low-income members have PRGF arrangements,[8] this would be an important channel. Using such augmentation of the PRGF would subsidise liquidity support for low-income countries. Augmentation of PRGF has been the main vehicle the Fund has used to provide financing for low-income countries hit by shocks. However, as the IMF itself recognises clearly, 'the small size and infrequency of PRGF arrangements suggests that there may be room for a more systematic response'.[9]

For low-income countries that do not have PRGF arrangements, but are eligible (around half), there are a number of options for financing shocks outside their control ('silent crises'): these options have been amply discussed recently in the IMF, but as yet very little action has been taken. One option would be to liberalise access to the CFF, liberalise its conditionality, and introduce a subsidy element into it for low-income countries.

Overall, the key point is for higher levels of IMF lending to be available for low-income countries, for this lending to have light or no conditionality – as such shocks are by definition exogenous – and for the lending to be subsidised. This would significantly reduce the negative impact of 'silent crises', which can have such a devastating impact on low-income countries' growth and poverty.

Increasing the Voice of Developing Countries in the IFIs

The case for increasing the voice of developing countries in the governance of IFIs is a compelling one. Current arrangements, with developing countries increasingly under-represented, are highly problematic for several reasons. First, inappropriate representation arrangements lead to a decline in the efficiency of these organizations, as decisions taken do not adequately reflect the needs and issues from the perspectives of the majority of the countries and peoples affected by them. Rustomjee gives several examples of inefficient outcomes linked to insufficient participation of developing countries in decision making in the IMF (for example in the design of Poverty Reduction Strategy Papers (PRSPs).

Second, insufficient representation of developing countries is increasingly perceived as leading to a democratic deficit in those institutions. Given that democratic governance has rightly emerged as such an important value in the last decade, and that developed country governments encourage democracy in developing countries, it is crucial that international finance governance is also democratic, as underlined by the Monterrey Consensus. This will be positive for the IFIs themselves, as it will clearly strengthen their legitimacy, which has been challenged in recent years. Therefore more democratic financial institutions would emerge as more legitimate and stronger ones.

Third, increasing the share of developing countries in IFI governance is necessary to help modernise the IFIs, so they reflect the increased importance of developing countries in the global economy, as well as the increased role of the IFIs in these countries. Thus, IFI governance has to better reflect today's new realities, rather than those that existed 60 years ago.

There is widespread recognition in the literature that necessary changes would include:

1 An increase in the share of basic votes, which is desirable to allow meaningful representation for smaller economies, as was established at Bretton Woods. Once increased, the share of basic votes should be maintained in future quota increases, to prevent similar future erosion. With the nearly 37-fold increase in quotas over the past 60 years, the share of basic votes in the IMF fell sharply, whilst IMF membership quadrupled. This has shifted the balance in favour of large economies.

The need to raise the share of basic votes is clearly a proposal that has obtained increased support, including the backing of some developed countries.

2 The quota formula needs amending to reflect the appropriately rapid growth of some developing economies, as the current quota structure does not reflect properly the scale of countries' economies.

3 There is a need to add at least one seat for African countries to the boards of the IMF and the World Bank. This would reduce the enormous burden and growth of workload in the two African constituencies, which represent jointly 45 countries, and would allow African Executive Directors to play a more active and effective role in broader policy discussions. This change would imply a very marginal increase in the size of the two boards or some very small reduction of European representation. Procedurally, it would be relatively easy to implement, as it does not require a change in the Articles of Agreement.

What Could Be the Way Forward?

To make such changes acceptable to industrial countries and to maintain the credibility of the IFIs in international capital markets, a compromise solution could be sought. This would attempt to achieve the above suggested three changes, in a way that would increase the overall voting share of developing countries fairly significantly, but would guarantee that – for a significant period, such as the next ten years – the voting share of developing countries in the IMF and World Bank boards would remain at below 50 per cent. Also, to make it politically feasible, it should maintain the veto power of the US and the EU. This would be a win–win situation for all parties, in that developing countries would see their share increased fairly significantly, but creditors would maintain their majority. The AAA status of the World Bank would be clearly assured (indeed, the regional banks maintain AAA status even when developing countries have a 50 per cent share of the votes on their boards).

It is important to note that Kelkar *et al.* have made a proposal for quota and voting power of the IMF Board that would precisely meet the above criteria. A similar proposal could be applied in the case of the World Bank. In the Kelkar *et al.* proposal, voting power would be determined by weighted averages for PPP–GDP (88.7 per cent) and basic votes at the historic ratio (11.3 per cent). This would mean that the voting share of developing countries would go up in the IMF from 30.5 to 42 per cent, thus clearly increasing their voice, whilst developed countries would reduce their voting share from 62 to 51 per cent, but maintain their majority.

Proposals such as the above could become the basis for constructive negotiations in the Development Committee and other appropriate fora. It would be valuable if developing countries could unite in support of such a formula. Jointly with progressive governments in the developed world, they could form an alliance for increasing the voice of developing countries in the IFIs.

Conclusions

The Monterrey Consensus expressed a concern about the lack of external finance to the majority of developing countries, especially low-income ones, and therefore highlighted the need for a substantial increase in both international official and private flows, if they are to achieve the Millennium Development Goals. Recent estimates presented in this chapter amply support the above concern. The chapter then discussed a number of current and new proposals for increasing both official and private flows to developing countries, particularly the poorer ones: the IFF proposed by the UK Treasury, public mechanisms to encourage private flows, especially towards infrastructure investment, and official liquidity facilities to help countries deal with external shocks, so that through reducing the burden of adjustment, they can have a more sustainable growth and a poverty-reducing path to enable them to meet the Millennium Development Goals. Finally, the chapter has offered a concrete proposal for increasing the voice of developing countries in the IFIs, so as to make them more responsive to the views and needs of developing countries.

5
Allocating a Global Levy
BOB DEACON

A progressive approach to globalisation will be distinct from neoliberal globalisation in developing a global social policy to complement and modify global economic policy. Social policy within one country embodies the three dimensions of social redistribution (from richer to poorer, from those at work to those not able to work, from one region to another), social regulation (to ensure that business activity does not contradict human needs) and social rights (to enable 'citizens' to access a reasonable degree of economic and social resources). Social policy within the most developed example of regional governance (the European Union) also provides for cross-border redistribution, cross-border social regulation and a cross-border declaration of social rights. Global social policy within the framework of a progressive globalisation will therefore aim to develop mechanisms for redistribution, regulation and the enhancement of social rights. Chapter 4 dealt with some proposals for global regulation. This chapter is concerned with global social redistribution within the framework of established international declarations concerned with social rights.

There has been considerable debate in recent years about the possibility of a global levy to fund an international programme of poverty alleviation and to augment or replace the problematic aid system. Most notably, a fully-fledged global campaign has now developed around the Tobin Tax, which would levy funds as a small percentage of international currency exchange transactions. Other ideas also exist, such as a tax on carbon emissions or as a simple percentage of GDP to be collected and provided by national governments. However, little thought has been given to how this new money might be spent or how international social transfers could take place. Even less thought has been given to what mechanisms for global resource allocation might be developed, who would decide, and on what criteria allocations would be made. Some initial answers to these questions are suggested below. How far these are developed in practice will be the outcome of a period of international and supranational debate and consensus building.

It is likely that steps towards a formal system of global redistribution that might eventually involve a Global Tax Authority and a Global Social Affairs Ministry will build upon, first, existing *ad hoc* mechanisms and, second, proposals for such mechanisms that are already within the global policy debate. Among existing mechanisms for international redistribution are the ones used by the Global Fund to Fight AIDS, TB and Malaria (www.theglobalfund.org). This fund uses a combination of criteria and mechanisms to allocate its resources where they are needed most in the world. Using the World Bank's categorisation of countries into low- and middle-income, the fund distinguishes between low-income countries who are fully eligible for monies and lower-middle-income countries who must match international funds with national funds and focus activities on the poor and vulnerable, aiming to be self-sufficient over time. A few upper-middle-income countries are also eligible in much the same way as lower-middle-income countries if they have exceptional need based on disease burden indicators.

The procedure used by this fund for allocating funds within the constraints above is based on a competition between bids from Country Coordinating Mechanisms (CCMs) within each eligible country. A partnership is aimed at between the global fund and national political effort that also embraces through the CCMs national partners drawn from the private sector, the professions and user groups. Where governments are non-functioning the applications can include non-governmental organisations. A board of internationally appointed technical experts adjudicate between competing applications using the following list of criteria: epidemiological and socio-economic indices, political commitment (of recipient governments), complementarity (to national effort), absorptive capacity (of governance mechanisms), soundness of project approach, feasibility, potential for sustainability, and whether or not there is a suitable evaluation and analysis mechanism. There are arguments for and against this responsive mode of resource allocation. Such an approach might miss the most needy, who are unable to bid, but it does involve a partnership between national and global effort. At the same time there is room for debate about the implicit conditionality built into the allocation mechanism. Good national governance is likely to be rewarded (except where it is recognised that no effective government exists). On the other hand a global fund that simply poured money into the coffers of a corrupt national government is likely to be criticised. All of the above criteria in various combinations are eminently suitable for decision making about the allocation of monies arising from our proposed global levy. They might be used either in response to bids or in the context of a top-down planning/allocation system. Details could vary depending on whether the monies were to be used for health, education or social protection purposes.

An idea on the drawing board and ready to be experimented with is that of the Global Social Trust Network.[10] It builds on the idea and practice, in many richer countries, of social partnerships within one country that fund social protection, and it seeks to extend this to develop international social partnerships between people in richer countries and those needing social protection in poorer countries. This global fund will be derived from resources voluntarily committed (at the suggested level of €5 a month or 0.2 per cent of monthly income) by individuals in OECD countries via the agency of social partner organisations such as trade unions or national social security funds. National Social Trust Organisations would then be established in both donor and recipient countries, and transfers would be organised through a global board with technical assistance provided in this case by the International Labour Organisation (ILO). Monies would then be spent by the National Social Trust Organisations in poorer countries, working through embryonic social protection mechanisms at local level. One suggestion is that the Global Social Trust Network would finance universal pensions at the level of one dollar a day. Pensions are recognised as being a very good cash benefit that actually meets the needs of whole families within extended family networks in poorer countries. The director of the Social Protection Network of the World Bank has commented favourably upon the ideas so long as the payments are linked to its Poverty Reduction Strategy Papers process.[11] This ensures that countries do not receive cheap loans from the Bank or have debt written off unless a public and transparent policy process has been established within the recipient country to reduce poverty. There is room for discussion as to whether the priority for international social protection expenditure should be old age pensions or, as favoured by Townsend,[12] universal child benefits. Any global levy could usefully provide additional resources to put into this Global Social Trust and thereby build upon the eloquent idea of the international social partnership embodied in it. The levy could also supplement incomes already being collected for other global funds such as those for cheap drugs or those for a World Water Contract.[13]

In addition to building on the practice of and complementing the emerging global funds discussed above, which seek to supplement national resources, a global levy would also make a major contribution to the realisation of the provision of global public goods and the prevention of global public bads. Sustained intellectual work being undertaken under the umbrella of the United Nations Development Programme (UNDP) by Inge Kaul and her colleagues[14] is now shaping a conception of global public goods that goes beyond the mere formal economist's criteria of goods that are technically non-excludable and non-rival in their consumption (world peace, for example) to embrace goods such as basic education and health care that are (or should be) 'socially determined public goods', which might be considered rival and excludable, but which by political decision could be regarded as non-exclusive. Political decisions about this could reflect the list of global social rights embodied within the 1967 UN Covenant on Economic, Cultural and Social Rights. Another approach would be to regard as socially determined global public goods those goods listed among the internationally agreed Millennium Development Goals being pursued by the UN Millennium Project Task Force. In other words, those things that benefit us all but no individual entrepreneur has an interest in providing – such as education and health in poor countries – should be considered as global public goods and an international effort should ensure their provision either by public service or privately in ways and with access criteria that enable all to benefit. A global levy could be used for such purposes.

Kaul and her colleagues make a useful distinction between development assistance, whereby richer countries donate monies to enable poorer countries to catch up in the development stakes, and global public goods.[15] Development assistance might continue in the context of progressive globalisation and could be provided with additional funds from the global levy. Additionally, mechanisms need to be set up to manage the provision of genuinely global public goods and diminish the existence of global public bads. Kaul and her colleagues envisage the establishment over time by each country of 'global issue ambassadors' located within international development departments. These ambassadors would work for policy coherence towards global issues across ministries such as trade and aid. There would be ambassadors for climate stability, food safety, international drug running, etcetera. National ambassadors would liaise with each other and develop international policy under the guidance of a global chief executive (for food safety, for example). Such a CEO would be advised by a global board drawn from relevant international organisations and be responsive to global civil society and global business interests.

This approach effectively adopts the networking and partnership form of global policy development and practice shifting, which involves collaboration between stakeholders in the international organisations, the global corporate sector, international NGOs and civil society organisations. Such a shift in the locus and substance of global policy making and practice has received support recently from commentators coming from very different intellectual positions. Rischard, the World Bank's vice-president for Europe, argues in *High Noon: 20 Global Issues and 20 Years to Solve Them*[16] that global multilateral institutions are not able to handle global issues on their own, that treaties and conventions are too slow for burning issues, that intergovernmental conferences do not have adequate follow-up mechanisms, and that the G7/G8 groupings are too exclusive.

Instead what is needed are global issues networks (GINs) involving governments, civil society and business, and facilitated by a multilateral organisation. GINs create a rough consensus about the problem to be solved and the goal to be achieved, establish norms and practice recommendations, and report on failing governments and encourage good practice through knowledge exchange and a global observatory to back a name-and-shame approach. Charlotte Streck in *Global Environmental Governance: Options and Opportunities* argues for global public policy networks (GPPNs)[17] which bring together governments, the private sector and civil society organisations. She insists that recent trends in international governance indicate that the focus has shifted from intergovernmental activity to multi-sectoral initiatives, from a largely formal legalistic approach to a less formal participatory and integrated approach. Such GPPNs can set agendas and standards, generate and disseminate knowledge, and bolster institutional effectiveness. Streck is building here on the work of Reinicke and Bennet, who argued that international organisations could play a particular role in GPPNs as conveners, platforms, networkers and sometimes partial financiers (see also www.gppi.net). If for now global policy making is likely to take this form, with global public goods being provided and global public bads being reduced through these mechanisms, then the global levy will provide useful additional revenues to this end.

In the long term, however, it is the aim of the progressive approach to globalisation to build support for a more systematic approach to global governance, especially in the social sphere. Those who argue for this[18] and those who only go along with the idea to a degree, and recognise that there are missing global institutions such as a tax authority,[19] all envisage either the creation within the UN system of an Economic and Social Security Council or a reformed Economic and Social Committee (ECOSOC) that will then assume responsibility for the steering of global social policy through the several UN agencies such as the World Health Organisation (WHO), the ILO, and the United Nations Educational, Social and Cultural Organisation (UNESCO), in collaboration with any residual functions still retained by the World Bank. In this future scenario the global levy will provide an additional and independent source of funding for all UN activity and the activity of its social agencies. In this case it is to be expected that several of the experimental global funds, such as those discussed earlier, and the several global issues networks reviewed above will be more firmly rooted within the UN system and be managed by a global council of ministers responsive to a global elected assembly.

There is one footnote to these proposals for spending a global levy that requires serious consideration. It is conceivable that, because of the opposition by the world superpower to any kind of global levy and any strengthening of the UN system, an alternative route to more systematic global governance might need to be considered in the concept of a strengthened 'regionalism with a social dimension'.[20] Within this scenario the EU would be joined by ASEAN, the Southern African Development Community (SADC), Mercosur, the South Asian Association for Regional Co-operation (SAARC) and new regions in a global federation of regions linked to, say, the Group of Twenty (G20) international governance mechanism. In this case a global levy would be allocated on socio-economic criteria of need to some regions, who would then decide to allocate it to activities and projects within the region using mechanisms already established by the EU or new mechanisms such as those under consideration by the Global Fund to Fight AIDS/TB/Malaria.

6
A New Global Monetary Architecture

JAMES B. QUILLIGAN

In 1941, America and Great Britain began discussing a plan to prevent the kind of international trade and monetary chaos that had led to the rise of fascism and the Second World War. Both nations agreed on the need for a reconstruction bank to supply the war-torn countries of Europe and other ex-colonial nations with the credit necessary to purchase food and raw materials, and to ensure long-term development. But the US and Britain had different ideas for assuring global exchange rate stability and orderly balance-of-payments regimes following the war.

The world's first conference on economic cooperation was held at Bretton Woods, New Hampshire, in July 1944. As an emerging superpower with a huge export surplus, the US sought to maintain its favourable balance of trade by eliminating exchange and trade controls in the post-war economy. Harry Dexter White, the Assistant Secretary of the Treasury and head American negotiator, insisted on an international stabilisation fund to provide credit and payment adjustments to nations with trade deficits. In essence, the US wanted deficit nations to borrow and repay their debt through the adjustment of exchange rates. Nations would settle their global balances, not through an international reserve currency, but in US dollars, backed by and redeemable for gold.

Ravaged by depression and war, Great Britain understood the plight of poor nations seeking import credit and favoured a new international trading currency. John Maynard Keynes, the eminent economist and chief British negotiator, proposed an International Clearing Union – a broad system of barter through which global trading transactions would offset each other.

Since creditors would be required to pay interest on their holdings of surplus international currency, just as debtors pay interest on their outstanding loans, each nation would be obligated to clear its accounts and maintain a neutral balance, preventing the accumulation of surpluses or deficits.

Keynes's plan was rejected before the meeting started. Although he chaired the negotiations on the reconstruction bank, the agenda for discussion at Bretton Woods was largely set by the US. When Keynes made several last-minute proposals, the US again rejected his ideas, threatening to deny Britain a desperately needed loan if it did not sign the final accord. Out of duty to the impoverished people of Britain, his commitment to providing poor nations with the credit to pay for imports, his conviction that some type of global economic system was the best hope for avoiding a currency meltdown like that of the 1930s, and his desire to accommodate the new multilateralist views of H. D. White and the US State Department, Keynes signed the Bretton Woods agreement on behalf of Britain. The US proposals were adopted: the bank for economic reconstruction became the World Bank, and the fund for international exchange rate stability became the International Monetary Fund.

Rather than achieve equilibrium in trade through orderly credit and exchange rate adjustments, as America had hoped, the last six decades of Bretton Woods monetary policy have confirmed Keynes's worst fears. Trade conflict, persistent debt and monetary volatility are inevitably produced when nations are pressured into exporting more goods and services than they import, instead of maintaining balanced trade. As surplus nations build up savings of foreign reserves and withdraw these export earnings from circulation, they leave that potential purchasing power idle rather than using it to buy the products of nations with trade deficits.

As a result, deficit nations drain their own savings of foreign reserves and borrow from international banks to buy foreign goods. But they spend more for these imports and the repayment of interest on their loans than they earn on their exports. This leads to the depletion and transfer of natural resources, erosion of public services and infrastructure, deepening poverty, and monetary weakness in deficit nations. (America, with a cumulative trade deficit of $2,700 billion, is an exception to this vicious cycle because US dollars are the *de facto* global currency, comprising about 80 per cent of foreign exchange and 50 per cent of world trade, allowing America to cover its trade gap through international investment of those dollars back into US assets; but with its huge debt and declining dollar, the US may not avoid major monetary problems for long if investors shun dollars for euros or other currencies.)

As the Brandt Commission noted in *North–South: a Programme for Survival* (1980), without an effective adjustment mechanism, trade surpluses are misallocated and global demand is severely dampened. Though surplus nations are the ones most able to bear the burden of global trade imbalances by spending their unused credit for the goods of deficit nations, they have thus far lacked the political will and vision to create a self-adjusting trade and monetary system. Like Keynes, Willy Brandt and his economic panel believed that surplus nations must accept the responsibility to use their excess foreign exchange to clear payments imbalances, ensure global liquidity, and generate global economic expansion, enabling all nations to avoid deflation and prosper.

Governments must engage in a serious discussion on democratic coordination of the global economy before the world's current debt and monetary crises erupt into chaos. The following framework for an economic clearing system – which could be implemented in gradual steps – is based on Keynes's original plan, the proposals of the Brandt Commission and other recent ideas from the fields of global monetary reform and ecological economics.

Creating an International Clearing Union in the Twenty-first Century

The Clearing Union

The Clearing Union is a self-balancing global economic system. Membership is voluntary and open to nations that conform to equitable economic standards. Nations may withdraw with advance notice. In a preliminary series of negotiations to adjust the global economic balance of power, nations agree to debt relief and emergency assistance for the poorest nations, permanent elimination of trade tariffs and subsidies (except as allowed by the Global Environment and Trade Organisation or GETO – see below), and gradual demilitarisation. On that basis, nations may then agree to the following provisions by international treaty.

Exchange rate

Each nation sets the value of its own currency against a global trading unit, possible called the Gea (see *The Global Central Bank*, below), through a fixed but periodically adjustable exchange rate. National central banks are ensured liquidity in all foreign transactions with other national central banks. Local prices fluctuate in the domestic currency. Barter-type, complementary currencies may also be used in support of local jobs, food production, health-care and other community services. (A prototype of the Gea – the Special Drawing Right, or SDR – is currently issued by the IMF.)

Trade deficits

When a nation's exports become less competitive on global markets, it may experience a trade deficit (imports exceed exports). Trade deficit nations are guaranteed reliable and affordable access to credit through a Global Clearing Fund (see below). To increase exports to surplus nations and earn new international exchange, a nation with a trade deficit may also decide to devalue its currency, increase taxes, lower government spending, or create tariffs and subsidies within GETO guidelines (see *Global Reserve Index*, below). Such decisions cannot be imposed from outside but only made internally by each nation through its governmental obligation to balance imports and exports by the end of each fiscal year. If it does not do so, a trade deficit nation is required to make interest payments on its overdrawn accounts. Debtor nations, therefore, have a strong incentive to achieve a neutral trade balance and avoid paying these fees.

Trade surpluses

When its exports become more competitive on global markets, a nation may experience a trade surplus (exports exceed imports). Trade surplus nations are required to circulate their foreign exchange reserves, rather than hoarding them. To spend this surplus credit and increase demand for the exports of deficit nations, a nation with a trade surplus may decide to strengthen the value of its currency, allow capital export, decrease taxes, raise government spending, lower tariffs within GETO guidelines, or increase foreign direct investment. If a trade surplus nation fails to bring its imports and exports into balance by the end of each fiscal year, the excess will be cleared through a transfer of resources, technology, or grants to a Global Resource Pool (see below), and/or through a 'negative' interest fee (demurrage) paid to a Global Clearing Fund (see below). As in the case of debtor nations, creditor nations have a strong incentive to achieve a zero trade balance to minimise or avoid these transfers and charges.

The Global Resource Pool

The Global Resource Pool receives the excess technology, commodities and other goods from nations with excess surpluses. These resources are distributed by the Global Resource Pool to trade deficit nations in the form of mass transfers or grants. (The UNDP and an expanded International Development Assistance division of the World Bank would serve this purpose; other World Bank functions could be eliminated.)

The Global Environment and Trade Organisation

Since all environmental and trade agencies focus on production, commodity management, resource distribution and consumption, their viewpoints, however divergent, must be reconciled equitably within one international body. GETO is dedicated to eliminating trade barriers, fostering trade agreements, regulating corporations through licensing, monitoring natural resource capital and production values, adjusting international commodity stocks, ensuring local production of commodities, protecting workers' rights and wages, curbing pollution and global warming, and maintaining the environment by targeting resource production at or below sustainable levels. Tariffs and subsidies may be permitted only in deficit nations to protect emerging industries. (If the WTO cannot be broadened and restructured for the task, the UN Conference on Trade and Development (UNCTAD), the ILO, the UN Commission on Sustainable Development (CSD) and other environmental agencies could spearhead this new organisation.)

The Global Reserve Index

Based on input from the Global Resource Pool and GETO, a Global Reserve Index is created by an independent agency, comprised of scientists and economists. Satellites and other scientific measures track a 'basket' of 15–20 (renewable and non-renewable) resources, from which a global *sustainability rate* is calculated daily. This value, replacing the traditional 'interest rate', expresses the average potential availability of global resources, which varies according to shifting patterns in stocks, volume, production, ownership, distribution, consumption, pollution, and resource regeneration. (This could be organised by the UN.)

The Global Central Bank

Using data from the Global Reserve Index, a Global Central Bank issues an international trade currency, the Gea (global economic account), a neutral unit issued free from debt or credit. This currency does not replace domestic currencies, but is used in all trading between nations as the reserve basis for international settlement and exchange. The Gea is only accessible to central banks for keeping deposits at the Global Central Bank. Exporters receive Gea credits, importers spend Gea credits, and each nation attempts to maintain an equivalence between the two accounts on an annual basis. Since the value of the Gea fluctuates daily according to the global *sustainability rate* (unlike the traditional interest rate, which is set every few months), the resources of the planet are, in effect, the asset reserves of the Global Central Bank in real time. (The Global Central Bank is created by global agreement.)

The Global Clearing Fund

A Global Clearing Fund receives interest payments from trade deficit nations, as well as 'negative' interest payments from trade surplus nations. These funds are used to provide loans for deficit nations with balance-of-payments problems. Another fund may also be used to bolster the commodity prices of trade deficit nations as an international safeguard against deflation. (A restructured IMF could serve this role.)

The Global Commons Council

A Global Commons Council audits the finances of the foregoing global institutions. In addition, it oversees financing for the operation (but not the programme capitalisation) of those global agencies, as well as international peacekeeping operations. These funds are generated by small *transaction fees* on global corporations, international investment, foreign exchange, global trade, international airline tickets, maritime freight, ocean fishing, seabed mining, offshore oil and gas, global oil trading, satellite orbital parking spaces, electromagnetic spectrum usage, usage of hydrocarbons and exhaustible resources, and energy consumption. International funding of these global institutions and services ensures that they are not beholden to national interests. (This council would be comprised of 22 eminent world statesmen, in consultation with representatives of a newly formed Global People's Assembly.)

Benefits of an International Clearing Union

The establishment of an International Clearing Union has a variety of benefits, not only over the current global monetary system but also over other ways of stabilising the international economy. These are briefly outlined below.

Business and government

- Market pricing power and the supply–demand mechanism remain free and open, without external interference.

- National sovereignty is honoured and fully protected.

- The independent functions of business and governments are clearly defined: the role of business is to produce and trade, and the role of national governments is to adjust the trade imbalances created by business.

Exchange rates

- Nations maintain their own domestic currencies and set their own fiscal policies.

- Domestic exchange rates are stabilised and domestic purchasing power remains relatively stable.

- Exchange rates are transparently adjusted by variations in natural resource availability, providing an intrinsic measure or value of the global resources needed to sustain long-term economic growth.

- The linking of national currencies to global natural resources eliminates problems historically associated with fiat currencies (such as permanent debt, excessive monetary volatility, inflation, currency hegemony).

Trade deficit nations

- Nations rely on their own naturally generated resources and create their own financial capital.
- Borrowing does not entail persistent debt and nations become less dependent upon global capital.
- Exports are generated not to pay the interest on debt, but to restore the national balance of trade.

Trade surplus nations

- Domestic budgets are balanced as government spending is disciplined.
- Strong trading partners are ensured.
- National surpluses do not result in a lack of global demand.

Global Resource Pool

- Nations are obliged to produce for themselves to the extent possible, donating their surpluses to an international clearing house through which those resources are distributed where they are most needed.
- The resource pool eliminates foreign aid: recipient nations are no longer dependent on aid flows, and donor nations no longer exert bilateral political control over aid recipients.

Global Environment and Trade Organisation

- Environment and trade organisations create mutual goals and incentives to reconcile their differences.
- As overproduction by poor nations and overconsumption by rich nations are curbed, destruction of soil, water supplies and habitats is slowed.
- As export-based development shifts to local development, long-distance transportation of goods diminishes and global climate change is reduced.
- Global liquidity is supported as natural resources are stabilised and enhanced.

- With emphasis on recycling surpluses to generate demand, international trade becomes equitable.
- Protectionism is eliminated globally, although deficit nations may protect nascent industries in select cases.
- Banks and multinational corporations are regulated through licensing.
- Wage levels rise; the price and quality of goods also improve.

Global Reserve Index

- Domestic exchange rates are informed daily by the global sustainability rate, allowing national currencies to reflect the actual value of global resources.
- As the sustainability rate falls through natural resource depletion and productivity declines, consumers recognise their purchasing power is lower and reduce their consumption; as the sustainability rate rises, consumers recognise their purchasing power is greater and consume more.
- As global resource values, monetary policy, national currencies, commodity prices, and consumer incentives are aligned, the human and social quality of life is enhanced and the global environment is protected.

Global Central Bank

- Money is no longer created through the loans from commercial banks to developing nations and the export of their goods and services; money is created on the basis of the sustainability of global resources.
- The debt-based money supply is superseded by credit for mutual benefit.
- International currency speculation, monetary volatility and inflation are virtually eliminated.
- The volume of international currency and liquidity is adjusted to meet effective world demand.
- International trade currency allows individual nations to be under the obligation of the community of nations, avoiding the hegemony of a single country issuing an international unit of exchange.

Global Clearing Fund

- Excess credit finances the transactions of deficit nations that need credit.

- As the debt burden is shared by deficit and surplus nations, the liquidity of the international financial system is expanded, deflation is eliminated, and global demand is restored.

- Hyper-competitive market pressures are reduced, imposed liberalisation is superseded by democratic consent, and domestic monetary discipline creates a new national ethic.

- As nations become partners in development, international cooperation becomes a new standard.

Global Commons Council

- Global institutions and services are independently audited.

- An automatic revenue source for global organisations, not requiring national taxes or contributions, is ensured.

- Global institutions and services are independent of strategic control by individual nations.

- International peacekeeping is funded on a multilateral basis.

Conclusion

In total, this proposal may appear ambitious. While undoubtedly it is a plan for longer-term change, there is no reason why most of its constituent elements cannot be developed incrementally as each has its own rationale and benefits.

However, we should not be fooled into thinking that the International Clearing Union constitutes the imposition of institutional control on a spontaneous or free global arrangement. The current system, despite its chaotic workings and negative effects, was carefully designed and then forcefully implemented and adapted in the post-war period. The only difference between the modified post-war settlement that now exists and the

International Clearing Union is that the former was designed to work primarily in the interests of the world's newest superpower, while the modified version of the Keynes vision presented here would work in the interests of all.

Part 3
Building Global Democracy and Peace

7
Rethinking Democracy for a Global Age

DAVID HELD

From the late eighteenth century, democracy began to be thought of as the right of citizens to participate in the determination of their own future through the medium of elected representatives. This system of 'representative democracy' was celebrated as accountable, feasible and stable over great territories and timespans. Representative democracy was heralded, as James Mill wrote, 'as the grand discovery of modern times' in which 'the solution of all difficulties, both speculative and practical, would be found'.

However, it was only with the achievement of citizenship for all adults, men and women, that representative democracy took on its current familiar form: a cluster of institutions and rules permitting the broadest participation of citizens in the selection of representatives who alone can make decisions affecting the whole community.

The Problem of Representative Democracy

Built, as it was, upon the structures of the modern state, the development of representative democracy took place within a fairly delimited territory. Modern democratic theory and practice were based on the assumption that citizens could come to identify sufficiently with each other to think and act together with the common good in view. It was taken for granted that all the key elements of self-determination – the people, the extent of the franchise, the form and scope of representation, and the nature and meaning of consent – could be specified for a circumscribed territory.

As a consequence of this, clear-cut distinctions could be drawn between domestic and foreign affairs. The fates of different political communities may be intertwined, but the appropriate place for determining the foundation of 'national fate' was the national community itself. Thus, the key principles and practices of liberal democracy are associated almost exclusively with the principles and institutions of the sovereign state.

Accordingly, the heart of the system of democratic states can be characterised by a number of striking features based upon the distinction between domestic and foreign policy or internal and external affairs:

- democracy in nation states and non-democratic relations among states;
- the entrenchment of accountability and democratic legitimacy *inside* state boundaries and the pursuit of maximum political advantage *outside* such boundaries;
- democracy and citizenship rights for those regarded as 'insiders' and the frequent negation of these rights for those beyond their borders.

However, democratic principle is fundamentally based on the belief that those significantly affected by public decisions should have an equal opportunity to influence and shape them. The nature of today's global interconnectedness, however, challenges the restriction of democratic influence to national territories. For example, a decision to permit the harvesting of rainforests may contribute to ecological damage far beyond the borders that formally limit the responsibility of a given set of decision makers. A decision to build a nuclear plant near the frontiers of a neighbouring country is a decision likely to be taken without consulting those in the nearby country, despite the many risks for them. A decision by large US corporations such as IBM or Microsoft can have profound effects on economic opportunities in countries such as India, but it will in all likelihood be taken without consultation with those in far-off lands.

These relatively simple but topical examples raise awkward questions for democratic practice. To whom, in an age of globalisation, should key decision makers be accountable? It is tempting to extrapolate the principle of accountability to those whom a decision affects but the answer cannot be this simple. As Bob Keohane has noted, 'being affected cannot be sufficient to create a valid claim. If it were, virtually nothing could ever be done, since there would be so many requirements for consultation and even veto points'. A subtler approach is required.

Strong, Moderate and Weak Forces

If we think of the effect of powerful forces on people's lives, their impact can be divided into three categories: strong, moderate and weak. Strong effects involve an impact where vital needs or interests are affected (from health to housing), with fundamental consequences for people's life expectancy. If people's urgent needs remain unmet, their lives will be in danger. In this context, people are at risk of serious harm.

Moderate effects involve an impact where needs are affected in such a way that people's ability to participate in their community (in economic, cultural and political activities) is in question. If people's secondary needs are unmet they will not be able to participate fully in their communities and their potential for involvement in public and private life will remain unfulfilled. Their choices will be restricted or depleted. In this context, people are at risk of harm to their life opportunities. At stake here is the quality of life chances.

Weak effects involve an impact that affects particular lifestyles or the range of available consumption choices (from clothes to music). If people's lifestyle needs are unmet their ability to develop their lives and express themselves through diverse media will be thwarted. In this context, unmet need can lead to anxiety and frustration.

These categories are not watertight, but they provide some useful guidance. In the light of these considerations, we can argue that those whose life expectancy and life chances are strongly or moderately affected by social forces and processes ought to have a stake in the determination of the conditions and regulation of these, either directly or indirectly through political representatives. Democracy is best located when it is closest to and involves those whose life expectancy and life chances are determined by powerful entities, bringing the circles of stakeholders and decision makers closer together.

However, the argument for extending this consideration to decisions and processes that affect lifestyle needs is less compelling, since these are fundamentally questions of value and identity for communities to resolve for themselves. Whether McDonald's should be allowed access across China, or US media products given free range in Canada, are questions largely for those countries to resolve.

Decentralisation and Centralisation

This principle of allowing people a say over decisions that impact on their lives to strong or moderate degrees points to the necessity of both the decentralisation and the centralisation of political power. If decision making is decentralised as much as possible, it maximises the opportunity of each person to influence the social conditions that shape his or her life. But if the decisions at issue are translocal, transnational, or transregional, then political institutions need also to have a wider scope and framework of operation alongside their local base. In this context, the creation of diverse sites and levels of democratic fora may be unavoidable. It may be unavoidable, paradoxically, for the very same reasons as decentralisation is desirable: it creates the possibility of including people who are significantly affected by a political issue in a public sphere that now extends beyond the normal limits of the national community.

To summarise, we now have a principle for democratic governance that breaks with the old national limitations. It is a principle of inclusiveness for all affected strongly or moderately by a decision and of subsidiarity whereby decision making is decentralised as much as possible, maximising each person's opportunity to influence the social conditions that shape his or her life. Concomitantly, centralisation is favoured if, and only if, it is the necessary basis for avoiding the exclusion of persons who are strongly or moderately affected by a political decision or outcome.

Democratising Global Governance

To entrench the principle of inclusiveness and subsidiarity requires a strengthening of global governance and a resolve to address those challenges generated by cross-border processes and forces. This democratic multilateralism must recognise the complex processes of an interconnected world. It ought to view certain issues – such as housing, education and policing – as appropriate for geographically limited political spheres (the city, region or state), while seeing others – such as the environment, world health and global economic regulation – as requiring new, more extensive institutions to address them.

What implications does this have for institutional reform at the global level? Initially, the prospects of democratic multilateralism could be enhanced if the UN system actually lived up to its Charter. Among other things, this would mean pursuing measures to implement key elements of the rights Conventions, and enforcing the prohibition on the discretionary right to use force. However, while each move in this direction would be helpful, it would still represent, at best, a move towards a very incomplete form of accountability and justice in global politics. For the dynamics and logic of the current hierarchical interstate system (with the USA in pole position) would still allow massive disparities of power, and the accountability gaps between decision makers and decision takers would remain unbridged.

Thus a democratic multilateralism would need to establish an overarching network of democratic public fora, covering cities, nation states, regions and the wider transnational order. It would need to create an effective and accountable political, administrative and regulatory capacity at global and regional levels to complement those at national and local levels. This would require a number of developments.

- *The formation of an authoritative assembly of all states and agencies* – a reformed General Assembly of the United Nations, or a complement to it. The focus of a global assembly would be the examination of those pressing problems that are at the heart of concerns about life expectancy and life chances – health and disease, food supply and distribution, the debt burden of the developing world, global warming and the reduction of the risks of nuclear, chemical and biological warfare. Its task would be to lay down, in framework-setting law, the standards and institutions required to embed the rule of law, democratic principles, and the minimum conditions for human agency to flourish.

- *The creation where feasible of regional parliaments and governance structures* (for example, in Latin America and Africa) and the enhancement of the role of such bodies where they already exist (the European Union) in order that their decisions become recognised and accepted as legitimate independent sources of regional and international regulation.

- *The opening up of functional inter-governmental organisations* (IGOs) – such as the WTO, IMF and World Bank – to public examination and agenda setting. Not only should such bodies be transparent in their activities, but they should be open to public scrutiny (on the basis perhaps of elected supervisory bodies, or functional deliberative fora, representative of the diverse interests in their constituencies), and accountable to regional and global assemblies.

- *The establishment, where IGOs are currently weak and/or lacking in enforcement capability, of new mechanisms and organisations* – in the areas of the environment and social affairs, for example. The creation of new global governance structures with responsibility for addressing poverty, welfare and related issues is vital to offset the power and influence of market-oriented agencies such as the WTO and IMF.

- *The enhancement of the transparency and accountability of the organisations of national and transnational civil society*, addressing the potentially disturbing effects of those who are able to 'shout the loudest' and of the lack of clarity about the terms of engagement of non-state actors with IGOs and other leading political bodies. Experiments are necessary to find ways of improving the internal codes of conduct and modes of operation of non-state actors, on the one hand, and of advancing their capacity to be represented in IGOs and other leading political bodies concerned with global policy processes, on the other. Moreover, to avoid citizens of developed countries being unfairly represented twice in global politics (once through their governments and once through their NGOs) special attention and support needs to be given to enhancing the role of NGOs from developing countries.

- *The use of general referenda cutting across nations and nation states at regional or global levels* in the case of contested priorities concerning the implementation of core democratic concerns. These could involve many different kinds of referenda, including a cross-section of the public, and/or of targeted and significantly affected groups in a particular policy area, and/or of the policy makers and legislators of national parliaments.

In the long term, a democratic multilateralism must involve the development of administrative capacity and independent political resources at regional and global levels. It does not call for the diminution *per se* of state power and capacity across the globe. Rather, it seeks to entrench and develop political institutions at regional and global levels as a necessary supplement to those at the level of the state. This conception of politics is based on the recognition of the continuing significance of democratic nation states, while arguing for layers of democratic governance to address broader and more global questions.

The Global Assembly

Perhaps the most significant of the above reforms is the establishment of a democratic and accountable global assembly. However, agreement on the terms of reference of a global assembly would be difficult, to say the least, although there is no shortage of plausible schemes and models. Ultimately, its terms of reference and operating rules would need to command widespread agreement and, hence, ought to be generated in a stakeholder process of consensus building – a global constitutional convention – involving states, IGOs, international NGOs, citizen groups and social movements.

Three core issues would need to be addressed:

- Who is to be represented: governments or citizens?

- What is to be the principle of representation: one state, one vote; proportional representation; or a mixture of both?

- What is the proper scope of a global assembly, and what are its limits of action?

These are demanding questions that admit of a number of sound theoretical answers. The case for each would have to be considered and weighed in the context of the diversity of interests that would be brought to a global constitutional convention – for example, the inevitable differences that would emerge between the developed and developing countries on whether population size or economic strength, or a mixture of both, should count in the determination of the basis of representation. While the legitimacy and credibility of a new global assembly would depend on its being firmly grounded on the principle of consent and electoral inclusiveness, it is likely that any assembly in the foreseeable future would be constituted by compromises between theoretical ideas and practical constraints. Accordingly, rather than setting out blueprints for the nature and form of a global assembly, and its related agencies, it seems better to stress the importance of a legitimate process of consensus building in and through which these issues might be deliberated upon and settled.

8
Rethinking Peace, Security and Human Rights for a Global Age

MARTIN SHAW

We are in the middle of a long historical transition. Slowly the world divided between warring states and empires that our grandparents knew has been giving way to a world in which state power is internationalised, ordered more by law than war. Although social democrats and progressives always had internationalist goals, in the last century their main concern was with achieving social justice inside the separate national states. Twenty-first-century social democracy is concerned with global social justice – but for this to be practicable, social democracy must also devote its energies to extending and consolidating the lawful world order.

Some basic political and legal foundations for this order have already been created. The United Nations system, established after the Second World War, developed some of the fundamental institutions necessary for world peace and security as well as extending the framework of international law. Although representing states and based on their rights, in theory the UN set these in a legal and political context of international cooperation and responsibilities, including those to individuals enshrined in the 1948 Universal Declaration on Human Rights. The 1948 Genocide Convention, building on the Nuremberg Trials, established in principle that state leaders should be punished for gross violations of people's rights, while the 1949 Geneva Conventions extended civilians' protection from war. In the Security Council, the UN established a central institution for enforcing international order. With the spread of independent statehood across the world following decolonisation, the UN became more genuinely representative of the world as a whole.

Much of the progressive global challenge is to make these existing norms and institutions work effectively for global peace, security and human rights. The problem is that both big and small states pursue their own interests, often in disregard of international norms, and support global institutions only when they fit their particular interests. During the Cold War, the UN and international law were often neutralised by bloc rivalry. Since 1989, gross abuses committed by regimes in smaller states like Serbia have led to some improvements in the UN's attention to and response to human rights and regional peace and security issues. There have been many terrible failures of global response, however, as in Rwanda in 1994. Overall the UN's capacities remain weak and the political will of its members (to deal with states' abuses) uncertain.

In practice, the momentum for global order depends much on the priorities of the most powerful states, especially of the dominant West and above all the USA. The 9/11 catastrophe has focused security politics on the threat posed by international terrorism to global networks, particularly transportation. It has led to a *regressive globalisation*, however, in which international policing is extended, but real international criminal justice is undermined; authoritarian states are overthrown, but by war and without proper international authority; and the linkages of regime change and security with democracy and human rights are weakened. In this sort of global politics, of course, the connections of peace, security and rights with wider issues of economic and social justice are largely disregarded.

A progressive globalisation, in contrast, must aim to harness the input of the well-resourced democracies for a more principled agenda of change, which both consolidates and extends existing global norms and institutions. There are five main areas in which this agenda needs developing.

Human Rights

For progressives and social democrats, human rights are not an optional extra to a global policy driven by the economic and national security interests of powerful states – or indeed to policies of economic and social development. The principles developed by the United Nations and campaigned for by many non-governmental organisations are central to the global project. While there is always room for further discussion of the meaning and scope of human rights, the central challenge for global politics is to make them meaningful in the lives of the majority of the world's people. Far too many of them live under the shadows not only of political but also of economic, cultural and even familial tyranny. The freedoms to speak, communicate and organise, without fear of dispossession or violence, are fundamental to a meaningful global order.

We must therefore seek to embed human rights in global institutional frameworks. Just as the European Union has established meaningful human rights conditions for membership, the UN and each regional organisation outside Europe should ensure that all its member states meet its own human rights criteria in practice, as a condition of continuing participation. The UN will need, therefore, to build monitoring processes into its activities far more thoroughly. In promoting human rights, the UN will need to support local human rights organisations, as well as relying on global NGOs like Amnesty International and Human Rights Watch.

Likewise, security policies must be developed that are based consistently on human rights. The campaign against terrorism cannot excuse alliances with corrupt, repressive or military regimes, or give any government the right to suspend fundamental rights or judicial norms in the treatment of suspected terrorists. Social and economic progress is impossible unless fundamental rights are consistently upheld.

Democracy, Pluralism and National Rights

Democracy is fundamental to a safe and peaceful global order. The worldwide spread of parliamentary democracy has been one of the most hopeful signs of the years since the end of the Cold War: for the first time, the majority of the world's states are formally democratic. By themselves, however, electoral processes do not guarantee real democracy. In many newly democratising countries, corruption and abuse of power nullify electoral choice; democracy without real pluralism and human rights can be a hollow shell. Even in some established democracies, the concentration of real power can be a serious problem, allowing electoral processes to be manipulated in favour of incumbent leaders and parties.

Democracy also raises the problem, 'Who are the people?' The evolution of modern statehood has tended towards the situation of 'one people – one state', assuming that each people is entitled to its state. The Wilsonian doctrine of 'self-determination', adopted during the twentieth century by most liberals, social democrats and communists, has entrenched this belief. In almost all states, however, society is multi-ethnic to a greater or lesser degree. One group's self-determination may be another group's oppression. Recent experience of national self-determination in the Balkans and elsewhere has shown its potential to contribute to war and genocide.

Democracy is only viable within pluralist national entities that guarantee the rights of individuals and minorities. Such pluralist entities work best as part of internationalised frameworks, like the EU, in which minorities can see their situations as parts of a larger picture. It cannot be accepted, therefore, that democracy automatically leads to peace: we see pluralist democracy within developed international frameworks as most likely to work in this direction.

Peace and Disarmament

One of the prime lessons of the last century is the ease with which our technologically and politically advanced civilisation can degenerate into war. Any kind of violence represents an acute problem in complex modern societies: whether this violence is carried out by 'terrorists' or by advanced Western states. Directly or indirectly, violence sharpens future conflicts rather than resolving existing ones. Military means almost always cut across our human rights and democratic priorities.

While progressives should favour extensive political and legal intervention by global authorities in nation states, therefore, we should remain generally sceptical about the value of military intervention to end abuses, protect human rights and promote democracy. In particular, progressives should oppose the idea of 'pre-emptive' military action recently adopted in the USA, in which military power becomes the preferred (rather than last-resort) tool of achieving regime change and other political objectives. The unilateral use of force by one powerful state will only encourage others to believe that they also have the impunity to use force when and where it suits their interests. A dangerous aspect of the 'war on terrorism' has been the apparent licence it has provided to repressive governments to use force against their opponents.

In addition, the existing international legal constraints on the use of force – limited to self-defence and operations for international peace and security approved by the UN Security Council – should be strictly observed. The UN should develop a more consistent policy concerning the limited range of circumstances in which international military intervention should be authorised – for example, to prevent or halt immediate armed threats to large numbers of civilians. The UN should also develop its own standing forces, with standing contributions from member states, rather than remaining dependent on coalitions of the interested or willing in particular crises.

International Justice

The consolidation of international law enforcement is one of the small success stories of global politics in the last decade of the twentieth century. Spurred on by the failure of global and regional organisations to prevent war and genocide in places like Yugoslavia and Rwanda, the UN established the first international tribunals since those of Nuremberg and Tokyo in the 1940s to indict the perpetrators of war crimes in the new conflicts. The International Criminal Tribunal for former Yugoslavia (ICTY), in particular, has proved an effective forcing house of global justice. The Tribunal has managed to catch, try and in some cases convict and sentence many of the more significant political leaders, military and prison personnel responsible for large-scale atrocities.

The Tribunal has shown itself able to be impartial between the different armies, while still discriminating in identifying the balance of responsibility; likewise, it has clarified some of the relevant international law, for example defining rape as a crime against humanity. Its relative success stimulated the demand for the permanent International Criminal Court, which finally came into existence in 2002 (although it has yet to try any cases). Although no system of formal justice could fully address the terrible harm caused to so many people by extensive armed violence – and there has been a parallel growth in interest in other kinds of justice such as 'truth and reconciliation' processes – the consolidation of international justice is an important way of institutionalising a global order. By showing that even heads of state (like Chile's Pinochet and Serbia's Milosevic) can be tried, this kind of justice sends an unmistakable message that the powerful everywhere may ultimately be brought to account for their crimes.

The role of international criminal justice is a striking illustration of the difference between progressive and regressive globalists. Here is a partly neglected mode of global intervention that could have provided alternatives to recent wars – for example if the UN had set up, in the early 1990s, a tribunal to try Saddam Hussein for his crimes of international aggression and genocide; or if in 2001 it had set up a special tribunal to try the leaders of al-Qaida, responsible for the 9/11 attacks.

Internationalisation and Regionalisation

Progressive writers from Tom Paine and Immanuel Kant onwards have seen international federation as the basis of worldwide cooperation and the principal basis for a peaceful world order. At many points in the past two centuries, imperial rivalries and totalitarian regimes have blocked any serious progress in this direction. In the emerging global world, however, a great range of international institutions have been developed that lock together nation states in cooperative frameworks, enabling them to manage rivalries through legal and political means rather than by war.

We should seek to develop these cooperative international institutions both as bases of economic and social progress and as ways of entrenching peaceful international relations. Although far from perfect, the EU provides a useful model of how to link international cooperation and progressive developments at the national level, especially in consolidating national and regional democratic forms and managing ethnic–national tensions. The links between open markets, international political institutions, shared economic prosperity and social protection, which social democrats have tried to foster within the EU, provide a basis that could be extended fruitfully in other world regions.

However, this model will not easily be transplanted into regions with different histories and levels of economic and democratic development. To encourage similar patterns of cooperation and growth will require both political leadership in world institutions and the commitment of major economic resources by states in wealthy regions of the world.

Part 4
Creating Equitable Trade

9
Equitable Trade and Development
ALAN HUDSON*

Trade and Development

International trade could help to lift hundreds of millions of people in the developing world out of poverty, as well as improving the living standards of people in the developed world. If each of the major developing regions – Africa, East Asia, South Asia and Latin America – was to increase its share of world exports by one per cent, Oxfam estimates that the resulting gains in income could lift 128 million people out of poverty. In Africa alone, this increase in trade would generate $70 billion, approximately five times what the continent receives in aid.[21]

International trade has enabled some countries to trade their way out of poverty. Indeed no country has developed successfully by isolating itself from international trade. But despite their efforts to integrate into the global economy, many countries – particularly in sub-Saharan Africa – have seen few benefits from international trade. Trade barriers and subsidies deny poor countries the opportunity to trade, and when they are given that opportunity, many do not have the capacity to respond by producing additional goods for export.

Particularly since the World Trade Organisation's 2001 Doha ministerial meeting promised a 'development round' of trade negotiations, there has been much debate about how international trade can be made to work better for poverty reduction and wealth generation. The rhetoric of a

---

* Alan Hudson is writing in a personal capacity for this book.

'development round', promoted by the developed world, suggests that trade liberalisation – the dismantling of barriers to trade – will unleash more trade, which will increase the size of the global economy, generating resources that can be invested in economic development and poverty reduction. The role of the WTO is to provide a multilateral framework for trade liberalisation. On the resulting level playing field, all countries will have the same opportunities to trade, lifting themselves out of poverty and towards greater wealth.

The narrative of trade and development promoted by the rhetoric of a 'development round' is misleading in its simplicity. History shows that there is no simple path leading from trade liberalisation to increased trade volumes, growth and poverty reduction. Trade liberalisation can contribute indirectly to poverty reduction, but if – in return for access to the developed world's markets – developing countries have to surrender their autonomy to adopt trade policies appropriate to their level of development (so-called 'policy space'), then they will be hindered in their efforts to take advantage of the enhanced market access that liberalisation delivers. In addition, without the capacity to respond to new export opportunities, enhanced access to the developed world's markets will be a hollow victory for many developing countries, especially the poorest. A game played on a level playing field, between unequal players, will produce inequitable outcomes.

This chapter describes the system of international trade and trade rules, explaining why 'free trade' does not amount to equitable trade, and suggesting what needs to be done – at the WTO, and beyond – to make trade work better for poverty reduction.

International Trade Rules OK?

International trade links producers and consumers in different countries because they are looking for a good deal, and because the costs of producing a particular good or service vary from country to country, depending on the resources the country has. By enabling countries to specialise in the production of those goods that they are well placed to produce (comparative advantage), and to then trade these goods with countries producing other goods, international trade promotes the more efficient use of resources, and boosts the size of the global economy.

The system of international trade is characterised by massively unequal players. For instance, sugar producers in many developing countries compete with the well-organised and influential sugar lobby in Western Europe, which has the resources to influence the European Union's policies on the production of, and trade in, sugar. Consumers range from poor households in developing countries to governments that are able to spend tens of billions of dollars on military equipment. Such inequalities of resources and power, when they shape the rules of the game for international trade, are crucial.

National governments have long recognised the value of international trade. Trade can boost their countries' economic growth by encouraging specialisation and efficient resource use, competition, and the transfer of technology and knowledge. And, by taxing international trade through tariffs, governments can raise revenue. This introduces a familiar dilemma. Each country would like to maximise its gains from trade, enacting policies to support the growth of industries and firms within its borders. But if this is done in such a way as to limit trade across borders, then the gains that trade can bring will not be realised. Beggar-thy-neighbour policies are not a sound basis for international trade.

Governments seek to defend the interests that they represent, but are enmeshed in a world made more interdependent by trade and other processes of globalisation. Countries have responded to this interdependence by establishing rules of the game to govern international trade. As the successor to the General Agreement on Tariffs and Trade, since 1994 the WTO has been the body with primary responsibility for bringing together governments to design, administer and enforce the rules of the game for international trade.

All countries would prefer rules that constrain the actions of others, while allowing themselves maximum room to manoeuvre, thereby enabling them to capture a bigger share of the gains from international trade. The role of the WTO is to establish universal rules – a level playing field – and, as the WTO has moved beyond the traditional tariff-cutting agenda, to specify what sorts of trade-related practices and policies national governments can engage in. This is why the WTO has assumed such importance in discussions of international trade. The WTO is not the only rule-making body in international trade, but in bringing together nearly 150 countries, and with the power to enforce its rules, it is the most important. If the WTO's rules were supportive of poverty reduction and development, this would be an important step on the road to making trade more equitable and globalisation more progressive.

On the face of it, the WTO's rules are designed to protect the interests of all and to prevent the powerful riding roughshod over the weak. The WTO in this view produces an international public good; rules which foster an open and predictable system of international trade. Rules however, always have distributional consequences. Rules shape outcomes, and outcomes are what really matter. A rules-based system is desirable and necessary, but it is not sufficient for achieving equitable outcomes. The nature of the rules matters hugely. If the rules are set by powerful governments, then they are likely to favour the interests that they represent. The WTO's agreement on Trade-Related Intellectual Property Rights (TRIPs) is perhaps the starkest example of this. By enforcing the commodification of knowledge, with little attention paid to the needs of developing countries, the TRIPs agreement will limit poor countries' access to the technology – including seeds and medicines – that they need if they are to feed their peoples and tackle HIV/AIDS and other diseases. To put it simply, if trade is to be harnessed for poverty reduction, then the rules governing trade must be designed with this goal in mind.[22]

Currently the system of international trade is massively inequitable, with many poor countries failing to benefit from trade liberalisation. As a result of the previous round of WTO negotiations – the 'Uruguay Round' – sub-Saharan Africa actually lost out. At the conclusion of that round, the United Nations Development Programme reported that the less-developed countries (LDCs) would lose $600 million per year, and that sub-Saharan Africa would lose $1.2 billion per year as a result of the agreement.[23]

As regards the rules, whilst others are bound by them, major players such as the EU and the USA have been able to carve out exceptions. Such exceptions, which are contrary to the principles of the WTO, have enabled them to continue massive subsidies to their agricultural sectors. This has been to the detriment of developing countries, which ought to have a comparative advantage in agriculture, as well as consumers and taxpayers in the rich world, and is contrary to the WTO's rules. Nevertheless, the subsidies have continued, and were protected until 2003 from legal challenge at the WTO by a 'peace clause' that the EU and the USA demanded. In total, the developed world provides nearly $350 billion per year of support to its agricultural sectors, a sum greater than the gross domestic product of the whole of sub-Saharan Africa.

As regards rule-making processes, the rich world has continued to try to set the agenda, promoting its interests by advocating rules that will constrain developing countries and prise open their markets. At the WTO's fifth ministerial meeting in Cancun, Mexico, in September 2003, this was seen most clearly in the attempt by the EU to force developing countries to widen the agenda to include the 'Singapore Issues' – rules on investment, competition, trade facilitation, and government procurement. This was despite the fact that the previously agreed condition for moving forward with negotiations on these issues – an 'explicit consensus' to do so – was so manifestly absent.

Why 'Free Trade' Does Not Amount to Equitable Trade

The rhetoric of a 'development round' suggests that reducing the barriers to trade (liberalisation) will increase trade, and that this in turn will increase the size of the global economy, making more resources available for economic growth and poverty reduction. It follows from this understanding of international trade that reducing the barriers to trade is key. Rules for international trade – administered and enforced by the WTO – should encourage liberalisation. On the resulting level playing field, all countries will be able to prosper. In this view, equality of opportunity is what matters; free trade amounts to equitable trade.

Regrettably, things are not that simple. It is not simply a case of designing trade rules that foster sensible trade policies and in turn lead to trade, economic growth and poverty reduction.[24] The view that trade liberalisation will lead to economic growth and poverty reduction is based on unrealistic and excessively abstract models of its impacts. These models focus on predicting the aggregate gains from trade, with little attention paid to the distribution of the gains (and losses) from trade. In the absence of mechanisms to redistribute the gains from trade, this is important. For instance, the World Bank, a supporter of trade liberalisation, predicts that developing countries will enjoy 50 per cent of an increase of $335 billion in global income by 2015 as a result of trade liberalisation. But sub-Saharan Africa and South Asia will receive minimal net gains.[25] Within countries, too, the gains and losses from trade will be distributed unevenly and not necessarily in such a way as to reduce poverty. This is not an argument for the *status quo*, but it does mean that the losers need to be helped to cope with change, particularly if their support for liberalisation is to be secured, as it must be in a WTO where all countries theoretically have the right of veto.

The models used to support the 'free trade' narrative confuse cause and effect in their analysis of the relationship between trade liberalisation, economic growth and poverty reduction. Rather than trade liberalisation leading to development, the reality is that as countries get richer they tend to liberalise. In a related sleight of hand, models supporting trade liberalisation employ different meanings of trade 'openness', conflating volumes of trade (which are positively correlated with development, but which have many causes) with liberal trade policies (which are the things governments can control, but do not necessarily lead to more trade and development).[26]

A careful reading of the historical evidence reveals that there is no simple relationship between trade liberalisation and the economic growth needed for poverty reduction. Most developed countries – the UK, the USA, South Korea and Taiwan are examples – developed behind barriers that protected their infant industries. Times have changed, and protection may not be appropriate now, but it would be misleading to claim that all countries have developed through trade liberalisation. For some commentators, the developed world's current efforts to persuade developing countries to liberalise amount to 'kicking away the ladder of development'.[27]

More recent history also shows clearly that liberalisation does not necessarily lead to economic growth and poverty reduction. Haiti, Mali, Nepal, Peru and Zambia have all embarked on programmes of rapid liberalisation but failed to make progress in delivering poverty reduction. Other countries such as China, Mauritius and Vietnam have been much more cautious in their approach to liberalisation, and have been much more successful in reducing poverty. And Africa – having complied with the demands of the IMF, the World Bank and aid donors by engaging in widespread liberalisation over the last few decades – remains mired in poverty. There are other causes of Africa's poverty – corruption and poor governance – but the historical evidence, from Africa and elsewhere, suggests at the very least that liberalisation is not a straightforward route to development and poverty reduction. As the Prime Minister of Ethiopia put it to the UK's Parliamentary Committee on International Development: 'Some would argue that across-the-board and reciprocal trade liberalisation is the right thing. The economic reforms in Africa over the past 20 years have been guided by such a view. The results, I believe, can speak for themselves.'[28]

The relationship between trade liberalisation, economic growth and poverty reduction is complex and country-specific, with the global effects of trade liberalisation translated into national-level impacts by domestic economic structures and institutions. Many roads lead to poverty reduction, and liberalisation can lead to other destinations. If trade liberalisation were a reliable route to poverty reduction, then a blanket prescription of trade liberalisation would make some sense. But as the sequencing, timing and rate of liberalisation matter hugely, it would be a big mistake – as well as being profoundly anti-democratic – for the powerful players in international trade to determine how quickly the poorer countries should open their markets. As liberalisation can lead to diverse outcomes, a focus on process is not enough. Trade rules, trade policies and trade are not good or bad in themselves; they are a means to an end. Human development outcomes, with poverty reduction to the fore, must be the priority.[29]

If countries are to translate the enhanced market access that liberalisation brings into positive human development outcomes, they must have the space – subject to the proviso that their policies don't harm other countries – to adopt trade policies appropriate to their levels of development. Market access through liberalisation is important for developing countries, but it will not suffice, and must not be bought at the expense of policy space.[30] Appropriate trade policies, and measures to build the capacity of developing countries to respond to market access opportunities, are crucial if developing countries are to benefit from trade liberalisation.

To make trade work better for poverty reduction, reforms must be made at the WTO and beyond. The WTO, whilst managing the process of multilateral liberalisation, must allow developing countries sufficient space to adopt appropriate policies. A game played on a level playing field between unequal players, where the powerful set the rules, will not lead to equitable outcomes. Mechanisms must also be implemented – within or beyond the WTO, depending on what will work – to ensure that the losers from liberalisation are compensated. Beyond the WTO, developing countries must be encouraged and assisted to consider the poverty impacts of trade reform, and, if appropriate, to integrate trade reforms with their development strategies; and they must be provided with technical assistance and capacity building to enable them to respond to new trading opportunities. Multilateral trade rules can provide the opportunity for countries to trade their way out of poverty. But rules alone cannot ensure that developing countries achieve this.

Towards a Development-friendly WTO: Market Access, Flexible Rules and Governance

For countries with few resources, small markets and little power, a multilateral, rules-based framework for international trade is highly desirable. In the absence of such a framework, they would be trampled in bilateral deals or simply excluded. The WTO provides this rules-based framework. Despite its flaws, developing countries have seen participation in the WTO as a way of defending their interests. At Doha in November 2001, the WTO's members agreed to begin negotiations towards the conclusion of a 'development round'. Since then, the debate has revolved around just what a 'development round' means: what is the relationship between trade liberalisation and development; and – given the uneven distribution of the gains and losses from trade liberalisation – which countries' development are we most concerned to promote?

Of three essential elements to a 'development round', the first is development-friendly agreements on specific issues, including agriculture and market access for non-agricultural goods. As an aside here, it would make a great deal of economic sense for agreements to be pursued on liberalising the movement of workers, but as this is so politically contentious, this isn't currently on the agenda in any meaningful way.[31] Second, progress in making the WTO's rules more development-friendly should incorporate greater flexibility for developing countries, as well as providing them with enhanced market access. And third, improvements are needed to the functioning of the WTO, including more effective participation by developing countries so that they – not Northern publics or commentators, however well-intentioned they might be – have the final say on whether the round has amounted to a 'development round'.

Market access: agriculture and beyond

A development-friendly agreement on agriculture is the key. Agriculture is the most distorted sector and the most important issue for developing countries. Three quarters of the world's poor live in rural areas. Agriculture is the primary export-earner and employment sector for developing countries, and most especially for the LDCs. What applies to agriculture, applies to other sectors too; developing countries need better market access, and the ability to open their markets at a speed appropriate to their level of development. And those countries that will lose out from liberalisation must be provided with transitional assistance. Overall, in a 'development round' agreements should only be entered into if it can be shown that they are developmental priorities.

Much of the developed world, especially the EU and the USA, subsidises its agriculture, stimulating production, and then dumps the surplus on world markets. Dumped food depresses prices and reduces the incentive for farmers in developing countries to produce and sell their products, either domestically or through export to third countries. Small farmers in many developing countries are forced out of business as a result of the EU's outrageous sugar regime; cotton producers in West Africa are driven to the wall by the USA's and the EU's cotton subsidies; the Jamaican dairy sector is devastated by the dumping of skimmed milk

Figure 8.1 World Trade in Agriculture, Pre-liberalisation[32]

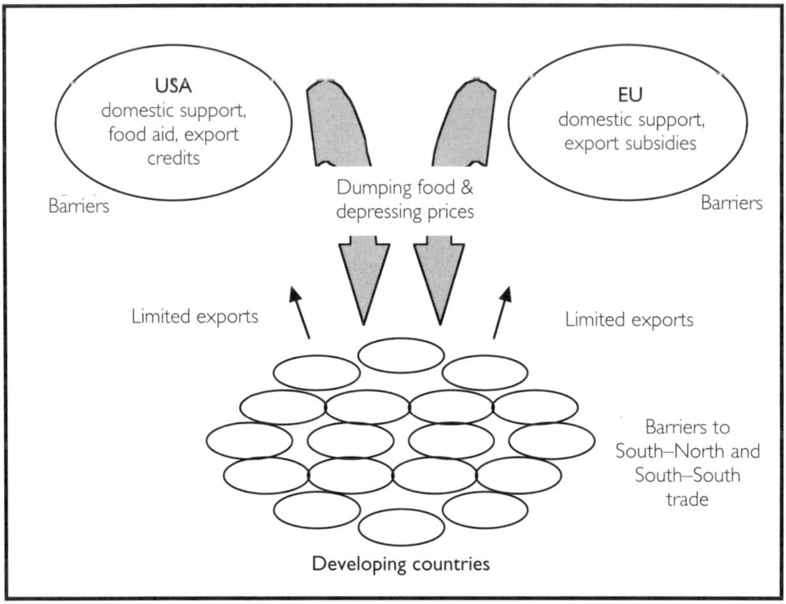

powder by the EU. The developed world also restricts access to its own markets by the imposition of high tariffs. Scandalously, these are focused on those products, such as beef, sugar and rice, that developing countries would like to be able to sell (so-called 'tariff peaks'), and are higher for processed goods than for raw materials, discouraging developing countries from adding value to their products (so-called 'tariff escalation').

Some developing countries – the net food-importing developing countries and countries that enjoy preferential access to the markets of the developed world – do benefit from the developed world's subsidies and protectionism, but overall there is no doubt that the agricultural policies pursued by the EU, the USA and other developed countries are disastrous for developing countries. And those countries that receive preferential access are not enabled to develop, they are simply trapped in a slightly less poor state than otherwise might be theirs. Market distortions make the playing field anything but level, and trap millions in avoidable poverty.

At Doha, the WTO's members committed themselves to establishing 'a fair and market-oriented trading system through a programme of fundamental reform'.[33] Members committed themselves to comprehensive negotiations aimed at substantial improvements in market access; reductions of (with a view to phasing out) all forms of export subsidies; and substantial reductions in trade-distorting domestic support. If the WTO's members honoured their Doha commitments on agriculture, this would be a major step towards securing a development-friendly outcome for the round as a whole. By making agriculture more responsive to market signals and less trade-distorting, such an outcome would reduce significantly North–South dumping of agricultural produce, and pave the way for increased South–North and South–South exports of agricultural goods.

There has been some progress, but not enough. Rather than seeking to work together to honour their Doha commitments, countries have done their best to concede as little as possible. Differences between countries in the EU bloc – primarily French foot-dragging – have watered down the EU's commitment to reform. Domestic political pressures in the USA have slowed progress, too. The EU and the USA seem keener to redefine agricultural subsidies, perhaps complying with the letter of WTO agreements, but certainly not honouring their spirit. Deadlines were missed in the lead-up to the Cancun ministerial meeting of September 2003, and no agreement was reached there. Eventually, in July 2004, a more modest agreement was reached, setting a framework for further negotiations but

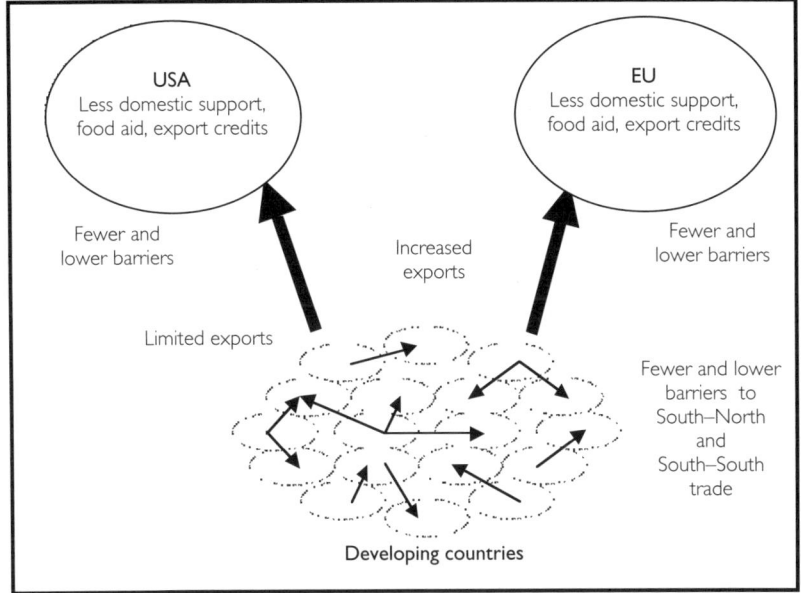

Figure 8.2 **World Trade in Agriculture, Post-liberalisation**[34]

not setting deadlines for reform. At the current rate of progress, the liberalisation of trade in agriculture will not make a real difference for at least another ten years.

If an agreement on agriculture is to be development-friendly, enabling poor countries to trade their way out of poverty, it must prevent the dumping of agricultural produce, and, in the meantime, it must allow developing countries to protect themselves from continued dumping. There should be a complete ban on the use of export subsidies, and on other ways of dumping food, and countries must not be permitted to subsidise their agricultural sectors at the expense of developing countries. In addition, tariffs should be reduced, and tariff peaks and escalation tackled. Duty- and quota-free access should be given to all LDC exports into developed countries, and countries benefiting from existing market distortions – the preference holders and the net food-importing developing countries – must be compensated and provided with assistance during the transition. For agriculture and for other issues, agreements should be assessed in terms of their likely development impacts.

One-size rules do not fit all: special and differential treatment and policy space for development

A key demand of developing countries is that the WTO's rules should be made more flexible, so that they can accommodate countries at different levels of development. So-called special and differential treatment (SDT) for developing countries is not a new feature of the multilateral trading system, but developed and developing countries agree that it has not worked well. At Doha in 2001, the WTO's members committed themselves to making SDT work better.

In the year following Doha, more than 80 proposals to improve SDT were submitted by developing countries, including proposals on preferential market access, policy space, the provision of financial and technical assistance, and proposals to make SDT mandatory and legally binding. Progress on adopting these proposals has been slow. Just under a third of the proposals have been provisionally agreed, but few if any of these have any real development value.

Perhaps the most contentious issue relating to SDT is developing countries' demand for their policy space to be protected. Policy space is sovereignty; a country's right to pursue within its borders policies that it has chosen to adopt. All countries have the right to policy space, the right to set domestic regulations: to protect infant industries, to promote rural development and food security, or to require outside investors to work with local firms. But in a globalising world in which domestic policies have international impacts, it may be necessary to constrain individual countries' policy space for the international collective good; this is why global governance, and the WTO as an institution of global governance matter.

The key questions are: how much policy space do (which) developing countries need; how much policy space can developing countries be given without one country's use of its policy space having an undue impact on another; and how can the WTO provide policy space and flexible rules whilst preserving the multilateral trading system? These are big and important questions, to which there are no easy answers, but as the Harvard economist Dani Rodrik has argued persuasively, if development really mattered, the role of the WTO would be one of managing the interface between different national systems and policy spaces, rather than reducing such institutional differences.[35] And a development-friendly

WTO would certainly not operate by requiring developing countries to surrender their policy space in return for enhanced market access. This was the putative 'Singapore Issues for Agriculture' deal at Cancun. Policy space can enable developing countries to respond to market access. To remove it, just when they need it, is crazy at best. In issue areas where there is a tension between developing countries' demands for flexibility, and developed countries' desire for universal rules, perhaps the answer is for the WTO not to over-extend its regulatory reach too far behind the borders of its members, and, for issues where universal rules are deemed desirable, to ensure that they are flexible enough to accommodate the needs of developing countries.

There is no straightforward path from trade liberalisation – via trade policies, trade volumes and economic growth – to poverty reduction. Given this fact, and the importance of locally appropriate institutions – not to mention the need for policies to be locally, preferably democratically, determined – developing countries' policy space must not be unduly constrained. The WTO, focused as it has become on the process of trade liberalisation rather than the outcome of sustainable development, is not an organisation one should readily trust to determine how much and what sort of policy space is needed for a country's development.

Putting development first? The WTO and the participation of developing countries

Two out of the last three WTO ministerial meetings – in Seattle and in Cancun – have ended in failure. This has raised serious questions about the way in which the WTO works and more specifically about its ability to deliver a 'development round'.[36] There is no room in this chapter to go into detail, but as the WTO is member-driven, and, at least on paper, is a one-member, one-vote organisation, the key to making the WTO more development-friendly must surely be to enable developing countries to participate more effectively. The UK government has done much to further this agenda. At Cancun developing countries came together in various groups – the G20, the G90 and the G33 – found their voices, and insisted that their voices be heard.[37] If they had not, they might well have found themselves signatories to a bad deal.

Several steps need to be taken to enable developing countries to participate still more effectively. First, more effort needs to be put into assessing and predicting the likely development impacts of trade agreements, and into enabling developing countries to work out what their interests are and how they are best promoted within the WTO. Second, developing countries need to be provided with the resources to enable them to participate effectively in WTO negotiations. Many poor countries barely have the capacity to keep up with negotiations. This is not helped when the WTO's agenda expands and timetables are tight. And third, the voice of developing countries must be heard. Getting agreement amongst 150 countries is no doubt demanding, but the participation of developing countries – something that is fundamental to equitable trade negotiations – must not be sacrificed in pursuit of speedier agreements. Mini-ministerials, secret negotiations at the WTO or 'Green Rooms' and plurilateral agreements that exclude developing countries all bring significant costs in terms of reduced democracy, transparency and accountability. Better trade-offs between efficiency and democracy must be found.

In a speech to the Fabian Society in June 2003, Patricia Hewitt, the Secretary of State for Trade and Industry, stated that the government 'will not accept any proposal we believe will damage the prospects of developing countries trading themselves out of poverty'.[38] In a 'development round', this is hardly radical; better would be a commitment to listen more carefully to developing countries' own determinations of their interests. If the UK had taken more seriously developing countries' opposition to the Singapore Issues before Cancun, and communicated this to the European Commission, perhaps the Commission might have been less stubborn in pressing – with disastrous consequences for the meeting's outcome – for the Singapore Issues' inclusion. By listening more, and helping developing countries to participate more effectively, the developed world can do much to make the WTO work better and be more development-friendly.

Beyond a Development-friendly WTO

The WTO – its agreements on specific issues, its rules, and the way it works – must be made more development-friendly. A multilateral rules-based framework for international trade is vital for developing countries, and, as rules have distributional consequences, it is crucial that such rules are supportive of development. But there is a tension between the way in which the WTO operates, through the trading of concessions, and the notion of a 'development round'. Many developing countries, and especially the poorest, have few if any concessions to trade, and little bargaining power. This does not mean that the developed world should be allowed to renege on its promise of a 'development round', but it does mean that there are limits to what such a process can achieve.

As careful analysis of the complex links between trade liberalisation and poverty reduction demonstrates, even if the WTO could establish a level playing field for international trade, and even if effective ways of providing flexibility within a universal framework of rules could be found, this would not be sufficient to make trade work for poverty reduction. More needs to be done, but not just at the WTO. Indeed, well-intentioned efforts to make the WTO pay more attention to development issues, if pushed too far, risk overloading the WTO with issues that it is ill-equipped to resolve. Reform at the WTO is crucial, but it is not the end of the story.[39]

Other than those who rightly call attention to the potentially harmful environmental impacts of international trade, almost all commentators believe that more trade is, in aggregate, a good thing. The concern from a development perspective is the fact that the gains (and the losses) from trade are distributed unevenly. In a WTO where each country has a veto, if agreements are to be reached, then all countries must expect to gain from trade agreements. If we are serious about making trade work for development, and securing trade agreements in support of this, then the answer is simple. The gains from trade should be redistributed so that all countries gain. That is, the losers from trade liberalisation should be provided with compensation or financial assistance to help them to cope with the changes that liberalisation will bring.

Sugar provides a good example. The sugar market as it now stands is massively distorted and inefficient. Tariffs, export subsidies and guaranteed prices result in sugar being grown in Northern Europe, a region whose comparative advantage surely does not lie in producing sugar, as well as in developing countries such as Barbados, Trinidad and Jamaica, where sugar is produced inefficiently, but which enjoy preferential access to the EU's markets. If the market were liberalised, and the distortions removed, only the efficient sugar producers would remain in business. The result would be not only that inefficient European sugar producers would go out of business, but also that inefficient developing country sugar producers – those which survived as a result of preferential access – would lose out too. By enhancing market access for all, liberalisation erodes the value of preferences. Efficient sugar producers such as Brazil, South Africa and Australia would be the main beneficiaries. This has led to some unholy alliances between the African, Caribbean and Pacific (ACP) countries that currently enjoy preferences and the EU; neither group has been in favour of liberalisation. If all countries are to endorse a liberalisation agenda, then those countries that will lose out – for instance the existing preference holders – must be guaranteed a share of the global gains from trade.

An important step in this direction was taken at Cancun, with the IMF proposing a 'contingent insurance' mechanism to help developing countries to cope with the costs of adjustment to liberalisation, including the loss of preferences and reduced tariff revenues. Given the IMF's track record of arm twisting in pursuit of liberalisation, and its intention to provide developing countries with additional loans rather than grants distributed from the gains from trade, the IMF might not be the best institution to administer such a fund, which should not be a sweetener to persuade countries to agree to fundamentally bad rules, but a means of persuading countries to agree to rules that may have short-term downsides. The design and operation of a compensation mechanism must involve developing countries and UN institutions such as UNDP and UNCTAD, which are more trusted by developing countries and have considerable experience in linking trade and development. And such a compensation mechanism must not – as happened during the Uruguay Round – be floated to persuade developing countries to support liberalisation, and then quietly dropped by the developed world. Indeed, some would argue that such a compensation mechanism must be integral to the WTO's agreements, and capable of enforcement through its dispute settlement mechanisms, for it to work.[40]

No matter whether such a compensation mechanism were administered by the WTO or another institution, making trade and trade liberalisation supportive of poverty reduction demands greater coherence between the various international institutions. Different organisations have different roles and mandates, but for the international system as a whole to promote poverty reduction in developing countries, these organisations must – without muddling their roles and overreaching their mandates – work together better. It is, for instance, counter-productive of development for the IMF to insist that developing countries liberalise their economies rapidly, while the WTO is granting such countries transition periods and policy space to prepare for liberalisation. Further, the purpose of coherence must be to promote development, and to make the multilateral system more supportive of developing countries' nationally determined development strategies; not to further the agendas of the developed world. Beyond compensation and adjustment assistance, there is a need to integrate trade reform and policy into poor countries' development strategies. The so-called Integrated Framework[41] offers some promise in this regard, but trade has been badly neglected in developing countries' Poverty Reduction Strategy Papers (PRSPs), and where it does form part of their strategies its likely uneven impacts on poverty are barely discussed. In a review of 17 PRSPs, only one included detailed analysis of the likely impact of trade policy on poverty.[42] Developing country governments, and the donors and international organisations that insist on developing countries producing PRSPs, have a responsibility to ensure that policy choices, including trade policy choices, are discussed widely, with poverty reduction prioritised. And when developing countries choose to make trade a part of their development strategies, donors such as the UK must ensure that aid is provided to enable developing countries to respond to the opportunities that trade liberalisation can bring. These days, the issue is not 'trade or aid?', but rather, 'how can aid be provided so that it enables countries to translate opportunities to trade into economic growth and poverty reduction?'

Overcoming the myopia that sees the WTO as the only game in town draws attention to other institutions and rules that shape the relationship between trade and development. First, attention must be given to the needs of commodity-dependent countries, which remain trapped in poverty and vulnerable to fluctuating world prices while still having to service considerable levels of debt. Second, bilateral and regional trade agreements must be supportive of development rather than an opportunity for the rich world either to exclude developing countries, or to twist their arms beyond the multilateral arena. Third, attention must be paid to the private sector too, and to the private rules that shape the relationship between trade and development. Internationally, there is a need to ensure that requirements such as the imposition of unnecessarily and unrealistically high standards for the export of agricultural produce do not exclude developing country exporters, replacing tariff barriers with other forms of protectionism, and that the corporate social responsibility agenda is pursued. Domestically, in developing countries, the private sector needs a business and investment climate in which it can prosper, driving the economic growth that is vital for poverty reduction.

Conclusions: Domestic Interests, International Repercussions

Trade can be a key element of progressive globalisation. But clarity as to the nature and purpose of progressive globalisation, and the relationship between trade and development is essential. If meeting the internationally agreed Millennium Development Goals is part of the purpose – as it surely must be – then international trade must be made to work better for poverty reduction. At the WTO, development-friendly agreements need to be secured, especially on agriculture; the framework of rules needs to be sufficiently flexible to accommodate countries at vastly disparate levels of development; and all countries need to be enabled to participate effectively. But this is only part of the story. A means of redistributing the gains from trade, to secure the support of the losers from liberalisation, is required. And developing countries should be encouraged to consider carefully the place of trade reform in their national strategies for development and poverty reduction, and assisted to take advantage of opportunities to trade.

There is much at stake for countries at all levels of development. If trade is a positive-sum game, then it can be a win–win game for all players. The resources generated by increased trade should allow countries in the North and South to pursue their priorities with more speed. In the developing world, tackling poverty is the priority. The developed world has also committed itself to working towards the Millennium Development Goals. Progress on poverty reduction would have major benefits for the developed world, too, going some way to breaking the link between poverty and global insecurity. And, not insignificantly, success with multilateralism in the trade sphere would demonstrate – not least to the USA – that working with others is more effective than working alone.

The British government has worked hard to make trade more supportive of poverty reduction, with the Department for International Development leading the way. But much remains to be done. The government needs to listen more to the concerns of developing countries, and transmit their views more forcefully to the EU. It needs to work harder to ensure that the balance of interests in the EU produces a real rather than a rhetorical commitment to a 'development round'. And it needs to continue its efforts to make the multilateral organisations – the WTO, the IMF, the World Bank and the United Nations – more effective players in the fight against global poverty, and to make them work better, and more coherently, together.

Coherence matters at home too. The UK has policies on many issues that relate to international development and poverty reduction: migration, arms exports, gender equality, agriculture and the environment, as well as trade. The government must – for reasons of efficiency if nothing else – ensure that such policy overlaps are made coherent rather than contradictory. It makes no sense to subsidise UK farmers if this undermines the effectiveness of policies on trade and development. Either change the objectives or change the policies. Similarly, if the welcome increases in overseas aid are to be well spent, they must go hand in hand with a determined effort to reform the system of international trade. It would be a massive waste of resources – taxpayers' resources – to provide developing countries with aid, on the one hand, and on the other to deny them access to trading opportunities. If they are to promote development, aid and trade must go hand-in-hand.

The UK government has demonstrated commendable commitment to international development and poverty reduction. And it has worked hard internationally to make trade work better for poverty reduction. But the pressure needs to be kept up. The government's performance on the international stage is driven in large part by the various domestic interests which it seeks to balance and represent. If we are to play our part in building a more inclusive and democratic system internationally, we must raise our voices domestically, signalling our strong support for equitable, fair and inclusive trade.

Part 5
Improving Global Regulation and Governance

10
Employment Regulation in a Global Economy

JOHN EVANS

Since the fall of the Berlin Wall and the emergence of China and India as major producers on world markets, the number of potential participants in the global trade and investment system has doubled from three to six billion people. The potential world labour force has also doubled. This initially impacted on the low-cost sectors of production and the workers employed in them, but technology is increasingly allowing the international comparative advantage also to have an effect in the service sector and on white-collar jobs previously thought immune to international relocation. Pressures on employment standards have therefore for the first time had a more generalised effect across different categories of jobs. Moreover, foreign investment now drives or operates in conjunction with trade – workers are confronted by the same firms, either directly as employers or indirectly through supply chains.

This issue therefore permeates significantly the daily relations between trade unions and employers. Employer attitudes towards unions generally – including policies on union recognition, labour costs, technological change and work organisation – are increasingly dictated by international competitiveness and international fashions. A whole business services industry to facilitate outsourcing is springing up. The threat of relocation to an offshore site is now the standard ploy in negotiations and in some cases has become the reality.

These pressures are greatest along the three North–South, East–West frontiers – Mexico–US, Central–Eastern Europe, China–East Asia. However, this is not just a North–South issue but affects both industrialised and developing countries. The rapid emergence of China, where low wages in most sectors are based on the suppression of union freedoms and workers' rights, as a major destination for foreign direct investment and now a member of the WTO, is having a chilling effect on the improvement of labour standards in East Asia and elsewhere. The most brutal examples of negative South–South competition to attract investment are often found in export-processing zones (EPZs) where semi-manufactured products or raw materials are processed into goods for export by foreign companies operating outside the normal laws and regulations of the host country. They may operate very differently in different parts of the world, but EPZs tend to have one overriding common characteristic: trade unions are tolerated in few, if any, of them. This is disturbing. An OECD report on trade and labour standards noted in 2000 that the number of EPZs worldwide had risen from some 500 in 1996 to about 850, not counting China's special economic zones. EPZs have become commonplace in many parts of Asia and Central America and are now spreading to Africa as a development model.

The result is a growing imbalance in the relative power of unions and employers in the labour market, while the regulatory role that governments were expected to fulfil is being undermined.

Enforceable Rules for the Global Labour Market

The progressive response cannot be to call for national borders and even European borders to be closed to flows of physical capital or goods. But nor can it be passive acceptance of the working of economists' 'relative price effect' in terms of labour, leading to a 'race to the bottom' in employment standards. We need a range of enforceable rules for global labour markets to ensure that certain basic issues are taken out of competition and that economic development sets in motion a 'race to the top' regarding employment standards.

The regulation of labour standards through the enforcement of certain global norms is not a 'new issue'. It has been part of the response to previous waves of globalisation: the creation of the ILO after the First World War; the Havana Charter and the attempt to create the International Trade Organisation after the Second World War. The current wave of globalisation has given the issue new focus.

The existing institutions and mechanisms of governance of global markets are imperfect. It is an admittedly simple truth that the institutions of social governance such as the ILO – which brings together labour and social affairs ministers and those responsible for human rights – are weak, whereas those that deal with property rights, such as the WTO or the international financial institutions, are strong. Moreover there is a lack of coherence between different parts of international governance. Governments can profess support for labour rights at the ILO while undermining these rights in their activities at the WTO. The UN system itself is facing reforms that it will take many years to deliver. So one has to be pragmatic and develop tools that work to meet the overall goals. This will involve different forms of regulation at different levels – local, national, regional and international.

A range of governance mechanisms is potentially available, from a set of 'hard' international regulations covering specific fields to looser policy coordination; regional integration; continuing national regulation; and even looser regional or district-level policies. While binding, 'hard' mechanisms of regulation at a global level will only be able to cover a limited number of areas such as fundamental rights. They are therefore not an alternative to the looser forms of coordination and cooperation in other areas.

A five-point strategy is needed to:

- guarantee fundamental human rights at the workplace through binding international regulation;
- establish enforceable intergovernmental regulation covering the accountability of corporations and their employment practices;
- create a negotiating space in international industrial regulations through the conclusion of global framework agreements between global union federations and multinational corporations;
- use market power such as the influence of workers' savings or consumer pressure to ensure that there is a viable business case for socially responsible investment;
- use the regional space for regulation created by the European process of regional integration.

Guaranteeing Fundamental Human Rights at Work

Globalisation has drawn dramatic attention to the need to guarantee core workers' rights on a global basis. The agreement in the ILO in 1998 of the Declaration on Fundamental Principles and Rights at Work, focusing on core rights (such as freedom of association, rights to collective bargaining, freedom from forced labour or prison labour, freedom from child labour exploitation and non-discrimination) has provided a floor for employment regulation in the global economy and a standard that should be applied throughout the international governance system. Such rights are vital to human dignity and self-respect in the workplace. These are fundamental requirements that have to apply before more extensive employment regulation can be implemented. Without respect for freedom of association it is hard to apply even basic labour or health and safety laws, or operate effective factory inspection. The core labour rights have also been agreed by the vast majority of countries operating in the global economy – the 177 members of the ILO – and it cannot be argued that they infringe upon national sovereignty. The issue is whether or not they are enforced in practice.

The international labour movement has long advocated workers' rights clauses in trade and investment agreements and in the constitution of the WTO. The idea of a workers' rights clause is to ensure that fundamental workers' rights embodied in the ILO Declaration on Fundamental Principles and Rights at Work become an integral part of trade agreements. This would require close cooperation on implementation between the WTO and the ILO. A workers' rights clause could make it easier for workers to form unions, and would ensure that all governments took serious measures to tackle abuse of basic workers' rights. It would provide a partial counterweight to the negative pressures on good labour relations in the global economy and could influence the behaviour of corporations.

However the issue has remained blocked in the WTO because of resistance from some developing countries and trade officials. If further trade liberalisation is to regain public support, WTO members must recognise that trade is only one of the pillars of sustainable development and give full attention to the social dimension of development, including respect for fundamental workers' rights. Greater democracy and transparency within the WTO will be required, along with progress on other key goals set by the Doha Development Agenda.

Other governmental institutions also have to treat core labour rights as criteria that they apply in their own activities. Both the G8 Labour Ministers meeting in Stuttgart in December 2003 and the ILO's World Commission on the Social Dimension of Globalisation have made strong pleas for far more attention to be paid to the social dimension of globalisation. Both have called for coherence to be established in the multilateral system to ensure respect for workers' rights by all international institutions, including the lending and conditionality policies of the IMF and World Bank as well as the WTO. The ILO Commission called for policy coherence initiatives by the different institutions and the establishment of a globalisation policy forum to establish coherence.

But action must go beyond strengthening dialogue and coherence to:

- continue to strengthen the ILO machinery for the ratification and supervision of core labour standards;
- defend the continued use of labour rights machinery in preferential trade arrangements;
- integrate obligations for core labour standards into all of the World Bank's lending policies;
- extend labour standards clauses in hemispheric and regional trade agreements;
- establish a forum to work on coherence between the ILO and the WTO;
- modernise Article XX of the GATT to exclude from WTO disciplines goods made by prison labour, extending this prohibition to any labour in abuse of core labour standards.

None of these propositions are revolutionary in nature, yet they are all attainable and their attainment would make a difference. Over time, with productivity growth, it would allow unions to 'bring the bottom up' in the global trade system.

Governmental Rules for Multinationals

Enforceable rules are also necessary to cover the activities of multinational enterprises. This has become mixed with the multifaceted initiatives of corporate social responsibility (CSR), where there is a contradiction between two governmental approaches. While some governments see the complexity of globalisation and a need for effective regulation, they realise that at the level of the nation state or even that of the European Union it is difficult to implement regulation of global markets. They therefore see CSR as a way of trying to achieve those public objectives in a global environment when more formal forms of regulation are impossible. But many governments also hide behind voluntarism and argue that if companies are prepared to take the responsibility for sustainable development and social and environmental standards, then there are fewer responsibilities for the state. The result is likely to lead to initiatives driven by public relations objectives and poorly enforced rather than effective regulation. Intergovernmental rules for multinationals do exist in the form of the OECD Guidelines on Multinational Enterprises and the ILO Tripartite Declaration of Principles Concerning Multinational Enterprises and Social Policy. Meanwhile, several NGOs are campaigning for a binding code on human rights to be adopted by the United Nations.

The OECD Guidelines on Multinational Enterprises were originally adopted in 1976 as a response to the involvement of certain US-based multinationals in the coup that overthrew President Allende of Chile. They were followed by the ILO's Tripartite Declaration and negotiations on the UN Code of Conduct for Transnational Corporations. These were eventually abandoned as the political tide turned with the election of the Thatcher and Reagan governments. However, a significant review took place in 2000. This was against the background of mounting public awareness, NGO criticism of multinationals, and the failure of the OECD to adopt the Multilateral Agreement on Investment. All this created a window of opportunity to transform the Guidelines into a more operational, more usable instrument that could be an important tool regulating employment in multinationals.

Although the Guidelines are not legally binding in the formal sense of international law, they nevertheless set out governmental expectations on how their companies (companies which are based and have their origins in the 38 signatory countries) should behave wherever they operate. They cover 85 per cent of global foreign direct investment. They are therefore not optional; they are political commitments by governments as to their expectations of the behaviour of their country's firms wherever they operate. There is a key difference between taking the attitude that an instrument is voluntary – so that it does not matter if you disobey it – and saying that it is a governmental expectation of what should be done.

The Guidelines specify the need to respect human rights and observe the core standards of the ILO, but they go a long way beyond this in terms of how companies are expected to operate: they set out prescriptions on union recognition, relative employment conditions, procedures for plant closures, and health and safety issues, to mention only a few elements.

Most importantly, however, the Guidelines have an enforcement mechanism, which is the new feature introduced by the review in 2000. Each signatory government is legally bound to establish a National Contact Point. The Contact Point is then expected, in addition to promotional activities, to receive cases and then try to conciliate between parties. If they cannot resolve cases successfully then they have to publish recommendations and put these in the public domain. The outcome should be that the company observes the Guidelines.

In the first three years following the review, some sixty cases have been raised with National Contact Points (NCPs). The cases cover a range of issues such as labour rights in developing and industrialised countries, plant closures and lack of information or lack of consultation before closures take place. A range of other issues have been raised by NGOs, in particular pertaining to environmental degradation and also to illegal activities of companies in the Democratic Republic of Congo amounting to the looting of scarce resources and raw materials. Of the 45 cases raised by trade unions about a dozen had been resolved by early 2004. The priority is to get more cases resolved positively. Some have been resolved through the active involvement of NCPs and others because a company did not want potentially bad publicity, but some have not been resolved and could not be resolved because governments do not take their responsibilities seriously. A key priority is that more NCPs manage to deal effectively with cases if the Guidelines are to remain a living instrument.

It is also essential that future granting of public subsidies and export credit guarantees should be conditional on the observance of the OECD Guidelines. This idea has met with furious business opposition. Nevertheless seven OECD countries now require a company, when it receives export credits or investment guarantees, to notify the government that it is aware of the Guidelines. Further progress on the issue of conditionality is necessary.

The Guidelines are not an alternative to legal regulation of companies, workers' capital strategies or collective bargaining (dealt with elsewhere in this chapter) but they can be an important complement. In the end their effectiveness depends on whether governments take their responsibilities seriously and make sure that they have properly functioning NCPs. Trade unions and NGOs must also take their responsibilities seriously and make use of them.

Building International Industrial Relations

An international framework for social justice needs to include a framework for industrial relations. But just as the earliest trade unions and collective agreements preceded a national legal framework, so international industrial relations are evolving as multinationals become engaged in different forms of negotiations with international trade union organisations.

Even though individual companies or industries are not legally obliged to recognise trade union organisations or engage in negotiations at the international level, limited international social dialogue has already started, notably with individual enterprises. On the trade union side, structures already exist – the global union federations (GUFs) – that can form part of the basis for international industrial relations at both industry and company levels. Many GUFs have already established structures that deal with particular multinational enterprises, usually company councils. In Europe, the law also requires a more formal structure for consultation, as mentioned below.

Global framework agreements – formal agreements signed between a GUF and a multinational enterprise – are the next step. Nearly 30 agreements have been concluded since 1998. Unlike unilateral company initiatives, agreements are a way to resolve conflicts or problems before they become serious or damaging: they aim to create dialogue and a certain amount of confidence inside the relationship. Unlike campaigns and other public action, the intention is to implement common, agreed principles in a way that leads to conflicts being resolved or even anticipated. Whereas most CSR exercises are voluntary efforts – promises or claims – the adoption of framework agreements can be seen as the start of international collective bargaining.

Using Market and Investor Power

Some of the momentum behind the debate over CSR and socially responsible investment has resulted from the market pressures created by consumers seeking to avoid buying products or services from firms seen to have negative social or environment practices. An industry in itself has been created in the area of social rating, certification verification and labelling. Some of these initiatives are supported by unions and NGOs and may be valuable, but many also have risks.

In sectors such as clothing and textiles, trade unions cooperate actively in certification initiatives such as Social Accountability 8000; these include certification schemes in China, because there is no other way for independent trade unions to get into factories in China. Certification bodies influence whether purchasers boycott products from certain factories. Trade unions have to be involved in what they are doing. On the other hand, some certification schemes can be misleading when information cannot be validated and verified properly. Inspectors may be present one day in a year but can't verify what happens on the other 364 days in the factory. A pragmatic approach to each instrument is needed to make sure that they are not mere public relations tools.

Market pressure for decent employment standards has also come from investors' concern over the potential risk of unsustainable social or environmental performance by companies in which they invest. With the collapse of ENRON and other corporate governance scandals the quality of corporate governance has become a key issue for investors.

A major campaign has developed in the trade union movement to mobilise the market pressure that potentially exists in workers' pension funds. Although retirement systems differ greatly between countries, an increasing number of them are using private funds as one of the ways to provide for retirement. The money is being invested in many different ways. Equity prices in industrial countries rose strongly in the 1990s, and more and more countries have stock markets: the importance of investment in stocks has grown accordingly. As a result of this, institutional investors, such as pension funds, own more and more shares in companies worldwide. And as workers, in turn, own these pension funds, they have indirectly become important investors in companies. The end result is that, as stockowners with voting power in a company, workers now may have an alternative course of action to change a company's behaviour.

The total assets of the world's pension funds reached almost US$13,500 billion at a first peak in 1999. After falling back to US$10,800 billion in 2002, assets grew again in 2003. The California Public Employees' Retirement System, the largest US public pension fund, had assets totalling over US$150 billion at the end of 2003 and managed pension and health benefits for more than 1.4 million Californian public employees, retirees and their families.

The International Confederation of Free Trade Unions (ICFTU), the Trade Union Advisory Committee of the Organisation for Economic Co-operation and Development (TUAC) and the GUFs have created an international network to facilitate cooperation on workers' capital strategies. Socially responsible investment – and in particular the behaviour of companies on workers' rights – is one of the main concerns of the Trade Union Advisory Committee. Companies are increasingly vulnerable to direct shareholder actions, and are therefore more and more concerned about their reputations. Trade unions have been very active over the last few years in initiating these shareholder actions. The Committee raises support at the international level for these campaigns. Executive remuneration has been, next to workers' rights, one of the re-emerging issues. Unocal, Haliburton, McDermott, Citigroup and Rio Tinto are just a few examples of companies that have been the subject of international trade union cooperation.

The many 'socially responsible' investment funds – funds that base their investment decisions on a specific set of social criteria – have also become important players. Furthermore, the issue has entered the mainstream investment world. For example, the UK, France and Germany now require their pension funds to disclose their policy on socially responsible investment.

There are also initiatives to improve information tools in which unions are participating such as the work of the Global Reporting Initiative (GRI) to establish and implement common international standards for corporate reporting on social and environmental sustainability.

Extending the Social Dimension of the European Union

The process of European political and economic integration has of course allowed cross-frontier regulation of labour standards to move well beyond the guarantee of core workers' rights. For many in Europe, the EU's 'Social Dimension' is *the* response to globalisation. The European trade union movement has sought (1) to establish a framework of standards to stop 'social dumping'; (2) to achieve progress in the harmonisation of social standards through both European legislation and social partner agreements; (3) to establish consultation, information and negotiation rights with multinational companies at a European level; (4) to expand the structural funds of the EU. One significant development in this process has been the passing of the European 'Works Council' Directive and the subsequent creation of more than seven hundred European Works Councils in the multinational companies operating across the EU. A further challenge is to link the European development to the global instruments described here.

Conclusion

If the 'social agenda' is to progress, the battle of ideas has to be won to show that it is possible to manage change in firms, industries, regions and labour markets in socially equitable ways. An industrial organisation model has to be developed which is both competitive and socially acceptable. OECD countries have to restructure on the basis of a high set of labour standards and not on the basis of a low-wage model of development, while developing countries have to ensure that productivity growth is used to raise living standards, reduce poverty and contribute to sustainable development.

The trade union movement is also having to become global in its reach. Assistance in capacity building and action on trade union rights and around multinational corporations is no longer perceived just as a form of 'solidarity', but rather as the necessary daily activity of unions. It is also worth remembering that we owe the growth of democracy in the world today not to global markets and entrepreneurs, but to workers who acted against repression and formed free trade unions in countries as diverse as Poland, South Africa, Korea and Brazil.

11
Protecting the Environment through Global Regulation

CRAIG BENNETT

For as long as they have been in existence, environmental organisations like Friends of the Earth have campaigned against the socially and environmentally destructive practices of companies. Over the years, activists have won campaigns against companies on a range of issues. Campaigning efforts have fuelled a significant growth in green consumerism, corporate social responsibility (CSR) and socially responsible investment (SRI). It is now almost impossible to find a large UK company that doesn't at least claim to care about social and environmental issues.

But little has really changed in the corporate world. There are an estimated 60,000 transnational corporations (TNCs)[43] and yet only a handful of these have CSR programmes. Many of these are incredibly superficial, serving primarily to create an *impression* of environmental and social good practice. And by creating this impression, companies have been able to argue quite successfully that there is no need for regulation in these areas. The level of political, academic and media support currently given to voluntary CSR far outweighs the change that has actually been delivered on the ground. Meanwhile, little attention is given to how those communities that have to live with the consequences of poor social and environmental performance might be able to seek justice.

Human rights, development and environmental organisations, trade unions, progressive think tanks and even some of the more enlightened sections of the corporate sector are now uniting behind the concept of corporate accountability. Instead of urging companies to voluntarily give an account of their activities and impacts, and voluntarily improve their social and environmental performance, the corporate accountability 'movement' believes corporations must be 'held to account' – implying enforceability.[44] There must be fundamental changes to the legal framework in which companies operate. These include social and environmental duties being placed on directors to counterbalance their existing duties on financial matters, and legal rights for local communities to seek compensation when they have suffered because directors have failed to uphold those duties.

This chapter will briefly review how the concept of corporate accountability has come about and how it is fundamentally different to voluntary CSR. I shall outline some of the mechanisms that could help deliver corporate accountability at the international level and at that of the EU, but I will also explore in some depth how the principles and components of these mechanisms could be transposed and made to work within one jurisdiction in particular – the UK.

From Corporate Campaigning to Campaigning for Corporate Accountability

Over the years, green groups have fought countless campaigns against companies over specific issues. They have forced companies to abandon plans to build roads, ports, mines, dams and pipelines in protected areas both here and abroad. They have bullied some high street banks into begrudgingly developing some limited expertise in environmental matters after we exposed how investors had been unwittingly financing rainforest clearance, human rights abuses and polluting industries. They have cajoled certain oil and gas companies into withdrawing from lobby groups set up specifically to stop governments from taking action on climate change.

Alongside this, green consumer campaigns have persuaded hundreds of thousands of shoppers to buy recycled paper, peat-free compost, fair trade and organic coffee, tea, chocolate and bananas, GM-free food, timber that has been certified as sustainable by the Forest Stewardship Council, and so on. Campaign groups have been able to expose the worst examples of corporate behaviour and indicate what kind of behaviour might be better. Green consumerism has shown that it is possible to make and sell products in an ethical way.

The Confederation of British Industries (CBI) recently said:

> Commercial opportunities have arisen for businesses to meet customer expectation of higher environmental standards, either as a core part of their brand or through *discrete* parts of their product range. For some, the beneficial effect on image and reputation of being environmentally proactive is also an important driver of behaviour.[45] [emphasis added]

The argument put by the CBI and others is that green consumerism and CSR have been so successful that a more regulatory approach is not necessary; the solution to environmental problems is the free market. Some, including ministers, are clearly so content with this neoliberal modus operandi that they have thanked NGOs for acting as the 'whistleblowers and enforcers'[46] and urged them to continue with their fine work.

While some may seek to perpetuate the view that green consumerism and CSR are somehow going to deliver in an adequate manner, there are very few campaigning organisations that share this perspective. The limits to green consumerism should be obvious. Greener products are often more expensive and represent a niche market compared to those products that are merely produced as cheaply as possible. A more fundamental limit is that even the most ardent, the most caring, the most affluent green consumer will never possess enough knowledge to buy ethically all the time. The average supermarket contains tens of thousands of product lines. Social and environmental issues are ever more complex and dynamic. How can we possibly expect consumers to keep abreast of all the latest developments and then have the time to work out for themselves what this mean for their shopping basket – in a world where people are increasingly time-poor?

The limits of CSR should also be obvious. There will never be enough NGO capacity to police the corporate world and run effective, inspiring campaigns to counter every type of corporate wrongdoing. The public, let alone the media, will never have the time or appetite for that number of campaigns. There are also countless companies that are not brand-sensitive, either because they are highly specialised or because they sell their products and services to other businesses, rather than to the public.[47]

More importantly, such a focus on the consumer and on the individual company ignores the real issues of social and environmental justice. Is it right for workers on banana plantations to suffer if, actually, the majority of Western consumers decide that having a cheap banana is more important to them than having a fairly traded banana? Is it right for Western governments to sit back and do nothing when indigenous communities get pushed off their land and rainforests are cleared to produce cheap palm oil for British supermarkets? Is it right for social and environmental concerns to be ignored in circumstances where addressing them does not make short-term business sense? Is it right for governments to surrender their responsibilities to govern, and rely instead on NGOs and the free market?

When our society decided it was time to mainstream common standards on health and safety and the protection of employees and consumers, it was done through changes to the legal framework in which companies operate. We gave company directors new legal duties and gave employees and consumers rights that would allow them to hold companies and directors to account if they failed to uphold those duties.

If we, as a society, are serious about sustainable development and social and environmental justice, the time has surely come to mainstream common standards on social and environmental performance. The way to do this is through equivalent changes to the legal framework that would allow people to hold corporations to account for social and environmental wrongdoing – corporate accountability.

These changes are already being campaigned for at the international, EU and UK levels. These campaigns differ in one crucial respect to those that have preceded them. Whereas, in the past, it was the corporations that were the target of the campaigners' strategies, the targets now are politicians and governments. This is because only politicians and governments can bring about the kind of legal changes advocated.

International Frameworks for Corporate Accountability

The last five years have seen a steady stream of proposals for mechanisms to deliver corporate accountability. The United Nations Research Institute for Social Development (UNRISD) recently offered the following summary:

> The emerging corporate accountability agenda includes proposals to establish institutional mechanisms that hold corporations to account, rather than simply

urging companies to improve standards or to report voluntarily. Corporate accountability initiatives promote complaints procedures, independent monitoring, compliance with national and international law and other agreed standards, mandatory reporting and redress for malpractice.

The corporate accountability movement has put the spotlight on certain issues that have not figured prominently, if at all, in the mainstream CSR agenda but which are fundamental to the role of TNCs in governance and development: corporate power; perverse fiscal, financial and pricing practices; and corporate lobbying for macroeconomic policies that can have negative developmental impacts.[48]

Some of these focus on specific sectors, such as the Framework Convention on Tobacco Control. Others focus on specific aspects of corporate accountability, such as the International Right to Know Campaign's call for disclosure and transparency. While sector-specific mechanisms will undoubtedly play a crucial role in delivering corporate accountability, there is a danger that they will only be developed for a handful of sectors.

In the run-up to the 2002 World Summit on Sustainable Development (frequently referred to as the 'Johannesburg Earth Summit'), Friends of the Earth International (FOEI) published proposals for a new international legally binding convention on corporate accountability and liability that sought to address problems common to the corporate sector as a whole. FOEI is the world's largest grassroots organisation, with member groups in 69 countries around the world. The proposal, developed by groups based in the global North, South, East and West, would impose the following requirements on signatory governments:

1 *Duties:* Impose duties on publicly traded companies, their directors and board-level officers to:

- report fully on their social and environmental impacts, on significant risks and on breaches of relevant standards (such reports to be independently verified);
- ensure effective prior consultations with affected communities, including the preparation of environmental impact assessments (EIAs) for significant activities and full public access to all relevant documentation; and
- take the negative social and environmental impacts of their activities fully into account in their corporate decision making.

2 *Liability:* Extend legal liability to directors for corporate breaches of national social and environmental laws, and to directors and corporations for corporate breaches of international laws or agreements.

3 *Rights of redress:* Guarantee legal rights of redress for citizens and communities adversely affected by corporate activities, including:
   - access for affected people anywhere in the world to pursue litigation where parent corporations claim a 'home', are domiciled or listed;
   - provision for legal challenge to company decisions by those with an interest;
   - a legal aid mechanism to provide public funds to support such challenges.

4 *Rights to resources:* Establish human and community rights of access to and control over the resources needed to enjoy a healthy and sustainable life, including rights
   - over common property resources and global commons such as forests, water, fisheries, genetic resources and minerals for indigenous peoples and local communities;
   - to prior consultation and veto over corporate projects, against displacement;
   - to compensation or reparation for resources expropriated by or for corporations.

5 *Standards:* Establish (and enforce) high minimum social, environmental, labour and human rights standards for corporate activities based, for example, on existing international agreements and reflecting the desirability of special and differential treatment for developing countries.

6 *Introduce sanctions:* Establish national legal provision for suitable sanctions for companies in breach of these new duties, rights and liabilities (wherever breaches occur) such as:
   - suspending national stock exchange listing;
   - withholding access for such companies to public subsidies, guarantees, loans or procurement contracts; and
   - in extreme cases the withdrawal of limited liability status.

7 *Extend the role of the International Criminal Court* to try directors and corporations for social, environmental and human rights crimes, perhaps involving a special tribunal for environmental abuses.

8 *Improve international monopoly controls* over mergers and monopolistic behaviour by corporations.

9 *Implementation mechanism:* Establish a continuing structure and process to monitor and review the implementation and effectiveness of the convention.

FOEI did not expect the Johannesburg Summit to result in a clear agreement to develop an international convention, let alone agree on its content. While the position paper contained some detail on how such a proposal would work in practice, it was not a draft convention.[49]

The purpose of the proposal was to provoke debate around the possible solutions to corporate wrongdoing, to promote a Southern agenda around community rights, as opposed to a Northern corporate agenda on voluntary codes of conduct, and to reverse the pendulum swing away from corporate voluntarism towards corporate accountability.

The call for corporate accountability became a rallying call for environment, human rights, development and labour organisations in the run-up to Johannesburg. Governments took note and a clear commitment was made at the meeting to develop new frameworks and mechanisms. This was summarised in the Final Plan of Implementation document which noted that 'urgent action' was required 'at all levels' to

> Actively promote corporate responsibility and accountability, based on the Rio Principles, including through the full development and effective implementation of intergovernmental agreements and measures, international initiatives and public–private partnerships, and appropriate national regulations, and support continuous improvement in corporate practices in all countries.[50]

Inevitably, different governments have differing opinions as to the meaning of this text. Governments from the G77 group of developing countries have consistently expressed their view that it calls for the development of new international frameworks. In contrast, the closing session of the Johannesburg Summit saw the USA declaring a formal 'reservation' with respect to the paragraph in which they noted their belief that it only referred to the development of 'existing agreements'.

The realisation of an International Convention on Corporate Accountability and Liability is clearly still some way off, but a long and slow process towards its realisation may have begun. An international framework represents the ultimate solution for many in the corporate accountability movement and one that many campaign groups continue to work towards.

EU Legislation for Corporate Accountability

The European Union is the world's largest single market and home to many of the world's largest corporations. If economic union is the *raison d'être* of the EU, then surely this needs to be paralleled by the development of mechanisms that ensure those corporations act in the interests of people and the environment, and allow stakeholders to hold EU-based corporations to account?

Recently, NGOs campaigning at European level – the Green 8 group of NGOs, the coalition of leading environmental groups engaged in the EU policy process[51] – participated in a two-year, multi-stakeholder process on CSR facilitated by the European Commission that concluded in June 2004. At the end of this process, the Green 8 issued a dissenting statement noting that the bias in the final report towards voluntary CSR was the result of a process that had been dominated by business interests.

They called on the European Commission, the Council and the Parliament to work together to develop a regulatory framework that ensures:

- mandatory corporate transparency on environmental and social performance and impacts;
- enforceable stakeholder rights to information, participation and accountability;
- public procurement and investment rules that discriminate in favour of companies whose responsible performance can be independently verified;
- clear standards and practices for the independent verification of corporate performance;
- tax reforms to internalise the environmental and social costs.

The most obvious way in which such measures could be introduced into EU legislation would be through a European Union Corporate Accountability and Liability Directive.

UK Legislation for Corporate Accountability

International conventions and EU directives must all be transposed into the domestic legislation of signatory/member states to come into force. To examine how such frameworks might work in a practical sense, it is necessary to explore in greater detail the technical and legal mechanisms that would facilitate their translation into national law.

In the UK, a coalition of NGOs, trade unions and think tanks known as the Corporate Responsibility Coalition (CORE)[52] has been developing proposals on how company law could be changed to hold UK companies to account. These proposals can be grouped under three headings:

1 Mandatory reporting and access to information

Legal requirements on companies to report annually on their financial performance form the basis of company law in most jurisdictions. A similar requirement on UK companies to report annually on their social and environmental performance is needed to form the basis of UK legislation for corporate accountability.

CORE would like to see a new legal duty placed on companies (or their directors) requiring them to report annually on the significant negative social and environmental impacts of their business operations, products, policies and procedures. There should be a requirement for these reports to be independently audited and for a range of key performance indicators (KPIs) to be developed to facilitate comparisons between companies and sectors.

2 New legal duties on company directors

UK company law already places a fiduciary duty on company directors, requiring them to act in the interest of the company and shareholders. This should be counterbalanced with new duties requiring directors to take reasonable steps to reduce the significant negative social and environmental impacts of their business operations, products, policies and procedures, which have been identified through the mandatory reporting requirements. This new duty could be referred to as a 'duty of care' to people and the environment.

3 New provisions for liability, including Foreign Direct Liability

Individuals or communities who suffer significant negative impacts because of the failure of UK companies (and directors) to have proper regard to these new duties, should be given the legal right to seek redress in a UK court, with legal aid. This would include negative impacts such as human rights and environmental abuses resulting directly from the operations, policies, products and procurement practices of UK companies or their overseas subsidiaries.

Under the approach adopted, it would be left to an aggrieved party or a prosecuting body to make a case in court that a company had failed to report on the 'significant' negative impact of its business policies, products, operations and procedures, or had failed to take 'reasonable' steps to reduce their negative impacts. The claimant would most likely point to evidence such as: more progressive behaviour being practised by a company's competitors; established and effective voluntary initiatives that the company had failed to participate in; expert witnesses; widely distributed research and materials, meaning the company should have been aware of a particular issue and impact; correspondence between interested, expert or affected parties; and so on.

Business lobby groups argue that regulating CSR would create a culture of compliance rather than innovation and tie business up in red tape. The reality is that the approach being developed by CORE does not represent 'red tape'. It wouldn't specify exactly how a company should go about improving its social and environmental performance, merely that it should. In the vast majority of circumstances, the way in which a company would do this is through a genuine CSR programme and/or by joining the relevant voluntary initiative and taking it seriously.

The CORE approach represents a statutory foundation for CSR, not a statutory straitjacket, and those companies that are genuine about improving their social and environmental performance would have nothing to lose and everything to gain.

Conclusion

Calls for mechanisms to deliver corporate accountability will continue to grow as the evidence mounts that voluntary CSR is failing to deliver the changes that are needed to deliver sustainable development and social and environmental justice.

The corporate accountability movement is far from having all the answers, but it has come a long way in a short time. Over the next few years, the debate and the campaigns will intensify. It is time for political parties, politicians and governments to join this debate and help develop the policies and mechanisms that will makes corporations fit for the twenty-first century.

12

An Equitable Approach to Migration

RUSSELL KING AND MARK THOMSON

We live in what has been called the 'age of migration'.[53] Yet it is useful to remember that in 2000 less than 3 per cent of the world's population – 175 million people – are officially recognised as international migrants, living in a country other than that of their birth.[54] Migrant numbers are rising, but only at a rate slightly faster than global population growth.

Statistics apart, it is often suggested that migration at the turn of the twenty-first century is qualitatively different. Globalisation helps to explain changes in the geography, forms and characteristics of migration today. Improved and more affordable transport and communication networks have made legal migration safer and more feasible. Globalisation has also brought greater interdependence between many migrant-sending and migrant-receiving countries: a growing number now rely on access to the 'global labour market', migrants' remittances bring much-needed foreign exchange to indebted national economies, and multinational companies indirectly promote migration by exposing developing countries to Western economic activities and lifestyles.

Yet the benefits of this globalisation of migration remain highly selective. Migrants are dichotomised: the 'desirable' and the 'rejected'. Developed countries compete on the global labour market for desirable, highly skilled workers, but resist opening up legal routes to less-skilled migrants. This has fuelled the business of traffickers and smuggling agents who reconcile the effective demand for flexible and cheap labour in developed countries with migrants' desire to leave their homeland. The decision to migrate, despite the huge legal and practical obstacles for some, indicates both the strength of labour demand in richer countries and lack of opportunities in poorer ones. Economic globalisation, imposed through the WTO, World Bank and IMF on many developing countries in the form of trade liberalisation and structural adjustment programmes, has left legacies of higher unemployment, lower living standards and cuts in social spending. Under such conditions, we can only speak of migration as a 'coping mechanism of last resort' for many individuals and their families.[55]

Developing an Equitable System of Migration

This brief introduction opens up four key issues that underpin our discussion of an equitable system of migration. First, developed countries are crucially implicated in the global dynamics of migration. Their central role in promoting international trade and finance on terms unfavourable to developing economies has widened global inequalities in wealth and increased outward migration pressures in many countries, particularly in sub-Saharan Africa.[56] These pressures affect both high- and low-skilled workers, but the costs (financial, physical and psychological) of migration fall much more heavily on those with fewer skills and from poorer socio-economic backgrounds. The reluctance of developed countries to expand legal routes for lower-skilled migrants, despite labour shortages in jobs shunned by the indigenous workforce, has not reduced migratory pressures. Instead, it has meant that transit and destination countries now host a growing number of undocumented immigrants whose 'illegal' status consigns them to a precarious life in the host society. A pertinent question, dealt with later, is why many of these countries tolerate the presence of 'unwanted immigrants' despite their hardline policy stances.[57]

Second, the growth in the smuggling and trafficking of migrants has altered the geography and politics of migration. Clandestine migratory routes have expanded into a number of transit countries, and border controls have been tightened to prevent immigration fraud and undocumented entry.[58] Popular discourses rightly highlight the exploitation of migrants that characterises trafficking, yet, in the view of many migrants, smugglers perform a vital service that enables them to escape poverty or, in the case of refugees, flee widespread violence and persecution. An equitable system of migration must provide migrants with alternatives to using smuggling agents or traffickers, including comprehensive information on new migration programmes that link labour shortages in one country to demand for work in another.

Third, the marginalised socio-economic position of many migrants in host countries must be acknowledged. Irregular migrants face poor pay, difficult or dangerous working conditions, inadequate housing and widespread discrimination. Parties with nationalist and racist agendas, particularly in Europe, have exploited fears about the unlawful presence of migrants. To argue that most fill labour shortages and contribute positively to the domestic economy appears ineffective in the face of persistent suspicion about migrants' reasons for immigrating, especially since September 11. An expansion of legal routes for less-skilled migrants would discourage many from working illegally or using the asylum system to delay deportation. Coupled with efforts to integrate migrants into the host society, community relations could certainly be improved.

There must also be the alternative for migrants to remain in their homeland. The financial cost alone to migrants of illegal migration raises questions about the plight of those who remain behind, including households who have invested savings and sold property to finance a family member's journey. It is also important to reiterate that the poorest and most vulnerable rarely have the option of migrating because of poor health, lack of information and limited financial means. A fourth key issue, therefore, in any vision of an equitable migration system must include joined-up policies linking migration to poverty alleviation and development in source countries. Concerns here centre on how migrants' remittances could be used to promote development in countries of origin, and how development might prevent 'brain drain' – the loss of their educated workers to more prosperous countries.

In summary, an equitable system of migration should include:

- an expansion of legal routes for lower-skilled migrants;

- new labour migration programmes providing migrants with comprehensive information on work opportunities abroad;

- opportunities for migrants to integrate into host societies;

- initiatives to link migration to development processes.

Expanding Legal Migration Routes

Migration policy in the developed world has emerged in an *ad hoc* fashion, but there has been a growing emphasis since the 1970s on immigration control. National governments have failed to recognise international migration as a feature of globalisation, and have instead treated migration policy in isolation from economic, social and demographic changes.[59] Even within states, coordination between government departments has been limited; the emphasis on controlling immigration has left little room for considering the economic need for migrant workers. Developed countries have consequently witnessed a growing divergence between the objectives of immigration policy and its outcomes.[60] The presence of undocumented migrants who fill domestic labour shortages indicates either that governments are unable to stem irregular flows of migrants, or that they are complicit in tolerating this source of cheap and flexible workers.

The latter explanation suggests a form of 'client politics', with businesses dependent on foreign workers able to form powerful lobbies to influence government.[61] If this is the case, governments risk condoning the exploitation of migrants, and encouraging growth in the number of undocumented, socially marginalised workers. Opening up legal migration routes for the lower-skilled would help address the problem of irregular migration in its various forms. Better pay and working conditions should be linked to an expansion of regular migration routes, whilst allowing social and economic ties to develop between countries of origin and destination. The view that this would create one-way migration to richer countries is not always empirically true. The act of regularising the status of undocumented migrants has allowed migrants in Europe to travel home, safe in the knowledge that they are legally entitled to return to the host country.

New Work Migration Programmes

Established ties between migrant-sending and migrant-receiving countries suggest that a system of managed migration is feasible – it should be remembered that most developed countries had immigration programmes in the decades following the Second World War. These ties often emerged from past or present colonial and economic activities, and then developed through the transnational practices of migrant households and businesses. What this reveals is significant patterning in the geography of international migration as pioneer migrations led to the departure of friends and families in a form of chain or network migration.[62] Although the process of globalisation has to some extent altered the geography of migration, migrants still tend to opt for the countries with which there are established ties and social networks. Indeed, recent research indicates that migrants initially follow established patterns of migration, but faced with discrimination and racism in their first destination of choice then travel on to another country.[63]

Existing labour migration programmes agreed between sending and receiving countries, and administered by the International Organisation for Migration, could provide a template for an expansion in programmes that build on existing ties between countries. Programmes would focus on providing impartial information to workers in source countries about job vacancies and legal routes of migration. Successful applicants would receive comprehensive information on their legal rights and obligations in the host society, be given support and advice on housing, education and training, and offered general social and cultural orientation. There should also be scope for involving various stakeholders in recruitment schemes, most obviously employers and local government, in order to support the integration of newly arrived migrants.

Integration

Integration of migrants must feature as a central aspect of managed migration; without this, migrants will continue to face widespread discrimination. Host societies should offer migrants information and support to help them adapt, access vital services, and avoid exploitation in the employment market. This information should also be available to migrants arriving outside the framework of migration programmes, including irregular workers. Undocumented migrants are easily exploited in the labour market, and the positions they fill create a functional reliance on cheap, flexible labour, particularly in certain sectors like the food industry and construction. Developed countries, by regularising migrants' status for at least one year, would send a signal to employers that exploitation of migrants is unacceptable, instead of presently targeting irregular workers – as opposed to their employers – in police checks and raids. Countries should also ratify the UN Convention on the Rights of Migrant Workers and their Families as a means to embody in domestic laws and practices the rights of migrants to decent working conditions, welfare services and family reunion.

Governments must take an active role in shifting the terms of public debate on immigration. There is also an urgent need to develop a pro-migrant stance in the mass media. Policy changes, notably the expansion of legal migration routes, will have to be debated and justified. The benefits of managed migration are not simply economic, and governments would be advised not to espouse immigration simply as a means to tackle labour shortages and ageing populations in developed countries. Migrants are not mere 'economic units', and treating them as such fosters socio-economic divisions between them and the indigenous workforce, especially during recessions. Opportunities to change jobs, enrol in education and settle in the host society must be available to migrants. Legitimising the presence of migrants is key to preventing long-term discrimination and exploitation, and to developing migration policies that are consistent with basic democratic principles. A policy emphasis on integration would bring closer interaction between migrants and the indigenous population, and help undermine prejudice and suspicion towards migrants.

Migration and Development

National and bilateral initiatives to facilitate integration and expand legal migration routes, however, do not address the inequalities between countries that induce migration in the first place. Equitable trade policies, public investment in healthcare and education, development aid and an end to global arms trading would significantly reduce migratory pressures. The objective, however, is not to stop migration, but to foster conditions in source countries that prevent migration becoming the only strategy to escape poverty. Multilateral initiatives, like the newly created Global Commission on Migration, have begun to focus on migration as a key development issue. But the 'migration–development nexus'[64] is complex, with varying effects over the short and long term. Certainly, emigration often results from low economic development and worsening social conditions at home; but the process of development can itself, at least for a time, raise levels of emigration as more people are able to access the 'migration route' out of poverty and as economic restructuring displaces labour-intensive operations, particularly in agriculture. Migration can stimulate development in formerly deprived regions through remittance of foreign earnings to the homeland. Global remittances account for significant capital flows to developing countries (US$88 billion in 2002), eclipsing the value of overseas development assistance (ODA). However, what form remittance-led development takes is crucial. Using remittances to build family homes or to pay for personal goods can induce further emigration by exposing others to the material benefits of migration. But if remittances are invested in businesses, communities are more likely to benefit from the proceeds of migration. If migrants are to invest in their home communities, then conditions there must be more favourable. The international community needs to commit resources to reducing poverty and the lack of opportunities in the developing world. Without this commitment, many countries will continue to face outward migration pressures, and will permanently lose many of their most educated and skilled workers to more prosperous countries.

Today, migration policy in the developed world consists of little more than cherry-picking highly skilled migrants, ostensibly in the name of 'fairer', more open immigration policies. Little concern is shown for the huge losses incurred by poorer nations that have invested a great deal in educating and training their workforce, only to witness the emigration of the most skilled. The developing world continues to suffer the effects of 'brain drain' – shortage of qualified people, falling standards in education and social services, weak infrastructure and limited prospects for business ventures. Sustained development would encourage skilled migrants to return home, but their return does not necessarily have to be permanent. An equitable system of migration should promote circular migration, so that migrants can travel and develop 'transnational ties' between the homeland and the host society. In this way, the higher incomes earned by migrants in richer countries have more 'value' when spent or invested in their home countries. Employment opportunities in more prosperous countries allow skilled migrants to learn new ideas, develop new skills and benefit from innovative technologies. But without channels to support the flow of skills, information and knowledge between migrant-sending and migrant-receiving countries, the developing world will continue to reap few benefits from the present system of migration.

Part 6
The Politics of Global Change

ADAM LENT

13
Building a Movement for Global Change

Building a movement for significant social, economic or political change is not straightforward. Activists and supporters often talk as though all that matters is a new vision, a more radical or a more moderate agenda, or the adoption of a specific tactical approach. In reality, genuinely effective movements are the result of a confluence of many factors, some of which, but not all, are well outside the control of movement leaders and supporters.

However, one thing is clear – a movement for change there must be. The forces shaping the global economy and politics in their image are so strong and inescapable that an agenda of the sort outlined in this book could never be achieved without a supportive countervailing force. One of the lessons of the social democratic transformation of Western Europe after 1945 was that politicians are only pressurised into or can only demand significant change when they are backed by a popular movement with a considerable degree of power to disrupt the normal run of politics, social relations and the economy.

The movement which achieved this in Europe was the labour movement in close alliance with social democratic parties across the continent. This movement took many decades to grow and faced many setbacks and some victories as it grew. This chapter will outline some of the key challenges facing any movement for global change built around the type of agenda detailed in this book if it is to grow and really bring about a lasting social democratic settlement for the globe.

Networks and Vision: The Crucial Dynamic

Any movement that has ever achieved any degree of significant and long-term popular backing has done so by recruiting members and supporters through pre-existing non-political networks. The labour movement did it through the factories that were established in the nineteenth and early twentieth centuries. The black civil rights movement was sustained by Christian churches in the southern states of America. Gay liberation and the women's movement spread through the expanded university sector of Western Europe and America in the 1960s and early 1970s. The debt cancellation campaign recruited support through churches, universities and development charities in the 1990s.

Such pre-existing networks are vital because they allow movements to target their appeal to a group with shared interests and/or values who are already meeting together as a collective. Effective movements will tailor their vision to suit the network they are addressing. In particular, the most effective and long-lasting movements will develop a message that combines the self-interest of their target network with a more idealistic vision of a better world for which the fulfilment of that self-interest is central.

Thus the labour movement, over many years, developed an appeal to the industrial working classes that closely aligned the achievement of better working conditions, pay and life chances with the creation of a socialist society from which all of humanity, or at least a whole nation, would benefit. Black civil rights combined the end of disenfranchisement of and discrimination against Southern blacks with a Christian vision of an America free of hatred and violence. Gay liberation and feminism combined sexual and social freedom for homosexuals and women with a vision of humanity liberated from sexual, class and gender repression.

This combination of self-interest and idealism is important, for each brings distinct strengths to a movement:

- Idealism alone is never enough to mobilise large numbers over reasonably long periods; some more virtuous types may need nothing more than the vision of a better world to suffer the various costs of political involvement; however, the majority are usually motivated, at least in the first instance, by the possibility of a better life or resistance to a worse one.

- Self-interest alone can sustain a movement but an idealistic vision can win a specific network and movement powerful allies in the form of intellectuals, politicians and the broader public. The idealistic dimension also allows other networks to consider how they might relate their own self-interest to an inspiring and persuasive vision, thus allowing the movement to grow in numbers and influence. An idealistic vision also stimulates within a movement the process of creating an identity and shared culture; this can be vital in maintaining unity, support and continuing recruitment, particularly in times of adversity.

However, not all networks and visions are created equal. The role that a network plays within a society can be central to the efficacy of the movement associated with it. In this regard, the labour movement had a vast advantage over all of the other movements mentioned here. The central role that factories and their associated transport and extractive sectors played in the economy of industrial society ensured that the disruptive potential of the labour movement was enormous. The capacity of organised workers to quite literally bring modern society to a halt gave them a rare power to demand and then ensure radical social and political change.

Which brings us to the current global justice movement. In the South, this is clearly a movement with a strong element of self-interest, appealing directly to those who have suffered as a result of the neoliberal policies detailed elsewhere in this book. The networks employed to build this movement have been workplaces, faith communities, educational institutions and a variety of other networks that differ from country to country.

What vision this movement propounds is less clear. In some places, it is socialist, in others 'localist'; elsewhere, it has a strong religious element. Maybe it will develop a greater consistency over time. However, the existence of strong networks, often with important economic roles and mobilised by self-interest, has provided the movement with a real power. On occasion this has been used to great disruptive effect, particularly in Latin America in recent years. They have even been mobilised to have significant, direct electoral impact, as in Brazil and in Venezuela.

However, the story in the North is very different. Here the movement is far weaker, despite some rather excited prognoses from the movement's own activists since the Seattle demonstrations. It is weak precisely because it is not involved in the dynamic of network and vision, of self-interest and idealism that is crucial for the most successful, effective and long-lasting movements.

Some strong networks have undoubtedly been involved in allowing the global justice movement to develop in recent years. Most notable have been the churches, universities and, most importantly, the aid agencies or development charities. It was this network that provided support and influence for the Jubilee debt campaign and, since then, a series of smaller 'anti-globalisation' campaigns particularly around opposition to trade liberalisation.

However, this is where the characteristics of success end and the problems begin for the global justice movement in the North.

- The foremost networks in the Northern movement have no significant social or economic role and hence their power to use or threaten serious disruption is very limited. The most they have been able to do is place politicians on the spot to explain why they are not living up to their own stated objectives or high moral tone, and/or to persuade the more sympathetic politicians to take some limited action. Of course, there have been some large demonstrations, some direct action and some eye-catching protests of other sorts, but the disruption has been very short-term, highly localised and ultimately easily resolved by authority through the use of harsher or innovative policing.

- There is no idealistic vision of change in any meaningful sense. Instead we have a moralistic appeal to mobilise and demand change on behalf of those in the South suffering from neoliberal policies. A genuine vision that does the three-way job of all good mobilising ideologies – identifies a problem confronting a community; explains the cause; and presents an alternative together with a plan for achieving it – is barely attempted. Indeed, rather than a genuine all-encompassing vision, the movement has offered a series of single-issue campaigns, with little attempt to explain their connection or broad resolution.

- The overwhelming moralism of this approach has ensured that there is no serious attempt to mobilise within networks by appealing to their self-interest. Beyond the rather vague claims that a more equitable global settlement might enhance the security from terrorist activity of Northern populations, there is little sustained argument that a major change in the nature of globalisation will benefit one or other specific network.

As a result, the Northern movement for global change *has* scored some significant political successes by mobilising large numbers within well-coordinated campaigns, but does not currently have the potential to bring about the type of sustained and profound change detailed in this book. It simply has not even begun to mobilise effectively within the types of non-political networks that have the power to effect significant social, political or economic disruption.

A Different Global Justice Movement

A truly effective Northern movement for global change would have a very different starting point from the current one. Its *raison d'être* would not be mobilisation of Northern populations on behalf of Southern populations. It would be designed to resolve the grievances of those in the North who have suffered as a result of the greater freedoms increasingly enjoyed by global corporations over the last forty years. Only with such a starting point can the movement operate in a context where it can sharpen its appeal to both the self-interest and the idealism of a support base.

Clearly, the most significant group in this regard is made up of employees working under conditions of weak job security and of hours and practices determined almost entirely by their employers. A movement that could once again bring politics to the workplace by explaining how the globalisation of the last forty years has removed the protections and influence employees once had would have the benefit, at least, of having identified a key network; it would be able to develop a vision in line with this book; and it would actually possess a group of supporters with the power to disrupt usual economic practice.

The agenda for such a movement would be less about the global as such and more about the personal in the context of the global. Instead of campaigning directly for a change to WTO rules, IMF policy or World Bank practices, it would campaign for a 35-hour week, the right to work flexibly or from home, affordable housing, a living wage and a living pension – issues that go to the heart of the self-interest of those employed in an economy where the corporations have the whiphand.

However, unlike the predominant political mode in the labour movement and on the traditional left, a global justice movement campaign around these goals would bring pressure to bear not on national governments and legislators alone but on the global corporations and institutions that have forced through the neoliberal policies of the last forty years and thus made labour market flexibility the norm to which all nations must aspire if they are to survive economically. In short, it is a movement that says: change the rules governing global corporations, not solely to benefit a Zambian farmer but also to benefit a British call-centre worker.

It is an approach that can also be seen in organisational terms as combining the targets and verve of the global justice movement with the bread-and-butter issues and networks of the trade union movement. This, however, leaves a gap. If such an agenda addresses the self-interest and networks of a necessary support base, where is the idealism? This is a more complex question. Self-interest itself is as much defined as discovered by a new movement; the idealism is even more subject to creation by the dynamics of an emerging movement. Thus, prediction is difficult when no such movement exists as yet in any meaningful sense.

This may seem a strange point to make at the end of a book that has been outlining a social democratic vision for the world. However, a hard intellectual task for all movements is developing an idealistic vision that flows naturally from the resolution of the self-interested grievances of the networks through which it recruits its support. Twentieth-century socialism and social democracy did this brilliantly by constructing the material well-being of the industrial working class as the cornerstone of the wider well-being of humanity. Much of this book, perhaps subconsciously, has continued this theme by constructing the material well-being of the new subaltern class – the poor of the South – as the cornerstone of that wider well-being.

Nevertheless, the whole thrust of this chapter has been to suggest that building a movement primarily around the self-interest of others – from the perspective of Northern populations – will never achieve success. Thus, the great intellectual task for social democracy must be to develop an idealistic vision that flows clearly and self-evidently from the Northern self-interest agenda outlined above. This, however, is a task to be completed elsewhere.

14
Conclusion: The Four Pillars of Progressive Global Change

The alternative approach to the neoliberal agenda outlined in this book is based on four pillars adapted from the history of social democracy for the new era of globalisation. These pillars and the key reforms they imply are listed below.

1 The creation of a new global economic settlement

- The establishment of an International Finance Facility as proposed by the UK Treasury.

- Greater use of public guarantees of investment in poor countries.

- More freely available loans from the IMF for low-income countries, particularly during periods of economic crisis.

- A stronger voice for poor countries within international financial institutions, including a fairer share of basic votes at the IMF and a seat for African countries on the boards of the IMF and World Bank.

In the longer term:

- The establishment of a global levy.

- The establishment of a formal system to distribute the receipts from a global levy.

- The establishment of an International Clearing Union to avoid imbalances in international trade.

2 *The establishment of a genuinely democratic system of global governance*

- The development of an authoritative world assembly of all states and agencies to address pressing global problems.

- The encouragement of regional parliaments and governance structures.

- The development of rigorous scrutiny of intergovernmental organisations by elected supervisory bodies.

- The establishment of new IGOs designed to address poverty and human welfare as a counter to the market-oriented approach of the WTO and IMF.

- The provision of more rights to NGOs to take part in the decision-making processes of IGOs.

- The use of cross-national referenda to address issues of international concern.

- The agreement of human rights 'thresholds' for membership of the United Nations and other international and regional organisations.

- The development of a consistent UN policy on international military intervention to defend human rights.

- The provision of strong international support for the work and principles of the International Criminal Court.

- The extension of the EU model of cooperation to other regions of the world: open markets, international political institutions, shared economic prosperity and social protection.

3 *The establishment of equitable trade*

- The negotiation of a genuinely development-friendly WTO including: (1) market access for agricultural goods from the developing world; (2) greater flexibility on market access for other goods; (3) more flexibility over 'policy space' for developing countries' governments in their trade policy; (4) more participation for the developing world in the WTO process; (5) more resources for the WTO representatives of developing countries; and (6) more analysis of the likely development impact of WTO decisions.

CONCLUSION

- The agreement of compensation for losers from trade liberalisation administered by trusted UN agencies.
- The integration of trade policy into the development strategies of poor countries.
- The provision of more attention in global trade policy to address the plight of commodity-dependent countries.
- Attention to be given to development issues in bilateral and regional trade agreements.

4 The establishment of enforceable rather than voluntary regulation of corporate and governmental action in the global sphere

On labour rights:

- The guarantee of fundamental human rights at the workplace through binding international regulation.
- The establishment of enforceable intergovernmental regulation covering the accountability of corporations and their employment practices.
- The creation of a negotiating space in international industrial regulations through the conclusion of global framework agreements between global union federations and multinational corporations.
- The use of market power such as the influence of workers' savings or consumer pressure to ensure that there is a viable business case for socially responsible investment.
- The use of the regional space for regulation created by the European process of regional integration.

On the environment:

- The imposition of duties on publicly traded companies, their directors and board level officers to: (1) report fully on their social and environmental impacts, on significant risks and on breaches of relevant standards (such reports to be independently verified); (2) ensure effective prior consultations with affected communities, including the preparation of environmental impact assessments for significant activities and full public access to all relevant documentation; and (3) take the negative social and environmental impacts of their activities fully into account in their corporate decision making.

- The extension of legal liability to directors for corporate breaches of national social and environmental laws, and to directors and corporations of corporate breaches of international laws or agreements.

- The guarantee of legal rights of redress for citizens and communities adversely affected by corporate activities, including: (1) access for affected people anywhere in the world to pursue litigation where parent corporations claim a 'home', are domiciled or listed; (2) provision for legal challenge to company decisions by those with an interest; and (3) a legal aid mechanism to provide public funds to support such challenges.

- The establishment of human and community rights of access to and control over the resources needed to enjoy a healthy and sustainable life, including rights (1) over common property resources and global commons such as forests, water, fisheries, genetic resources and minerals for indigenous peoples and local communities; (2) to prior consultation and veto over corporate projects, against displacement; and (3) to compensation or reparation for resources expropriated by or for corporations.

On migration:

- The expansion of legal routes for lower-skilled migrants.

- The establishment of new labour migration programmes providing migrants with comprehensive information on work opportunities abroad.

- The development of opportunities for migrants to integrate into host societies.

- The establishment of initiatives to link migration to development processes.

On the reform of company law:

- The reform of domestic company law to provide for: (1) legal requirements on companies to report annually on their social and environmental performance; (2) new duties requiring directors to take reasonable steps to reduce the significant negative social and environmental impacts of their business operations, products, policies and procedures; and (3) the legal right for individuals or communities to seek redress against a corporation in a court of the corporation's home country.

Notes

Chapter 2

1 A much more detailed account of this narrative can be found in Scott Newton, *The Global Economy 1944–2000*, London: Arnold, 2004.

Chapter 4

2 This chapter draws on a study prepared for the ACP Fourth Summit, held in Maputo in June 2004. We thank Adam Lent and Peter O'Brien for valuable suggestions.
3 Details on methodology and hypotheses used can be found in Gottschalk, R. (2004) 'How Much External Finance will be Needed to Meet the Poverty-reducing Target by 2015?' Paper prepared as part of the Comprehensive Evaluation of the African Development Fund 1996–2002.
4 The UN Millennium Project used a sectoral approach to calculate such needs. It looked at the financing needs in infrastructure, social service provision and human resources, for selected sub-Saharan African countries (see *Economist*, 22 May 2004).
5 HM Treasury and DFID (2003) 'International Finance Facility: a technical note', HM Treasury, February.
6 Griffith-Jones, S. and A. Fuzzo de Lima (2004) 'Alternative Loan Guarantee Mechanisms and Project Finance for Infrastructure in Developing Countries', available at www.ids.ac.uk/ids/global/Finance/ifpubs.html

7 Griffith-Jones, S. and J. A. Ocampo (2003) 'What Progress on International Financial Reform? Why So Limited?' Stockholm: GDI Study, p. 1.
 Oxfam (2003) 'The IMF and the Millennium Goals. Failing to Deliver for Low Income Countries', Oxfam Briefing Paper 54, September.
8 International Monetary Fund (2003) *Fund Assistance for Countries Facing Exogenous Shocks*, August, http://www.imf.org/external/np/pdr/sustain/2003/080803.pdf.
9 Ibid.

Chapter 5

10 Cichon, M. *et al.* (2003) *A Global Social Trust Network: a New Tool to Combat Poverty Through Social Protection*, Geneva: International Labour Organisation.
11 Holzmann, R. (2002) 'Interview' reported in Cichon *et al.*, *A Global Social Trust Network*, Geneva: International Labour Organisation.
12 Townsend, P. and D. Gordon (2002) *World Poverty: New Policies to Defeat an Old Enemy*, Bristol: Policy Press.
13 Petrella R. (2001) *The Water Manifesto: Arguments for a World Water Contract*, London: Zed Books.
14 Kaul, I. *et al.* (1999) *Global Public Goods: International Cooperation in the Twenty-first Century*, Oxford: Oxford University Press.
15 Kaul, I. *et al.* (2003) *Global Public Goods: Managing Globalisation*, Oxford: Oxford University Press, p. 358.
16 Rischard, J. F. (2002) *High Noon: Twenty Global Problems, Twenty Years to Solve Them*, Oxford: Perseus Books.
17 Streck, C. (2002) 'Global Public Policy Networks as Coalitions for Change', in D. Esty and M. H. Ivanova (eds.), *Global Environmental Governance: Options and Opportunities*, Yale: Yale University Press.
18 Held, D. and A. McGrew (2002) *Governing Globalisation: Power, Authority and Global Governance*, Cambridge: Polity Press; Patomaki, H. (1999) Democratising Globalisation: the Leverage of the Tobin Tax, London: Zed Books; Deacon, B. *et al.* (2003) *Global Social Governance: Themes and Prospects*, Helsinki: Finnish Ministry of Foreign Affairs.
19 Nayyer, D. (2002) *Governing Globalisation: Issues and Institutions*, Oxford: Oxford University Press.
20 Deacon, B. (2001) *The Social Dimension of Regionalism*, Helsinki: Stakes (www.gaspp.org)

Chapter 9

21 House of Commons International Development Committee, Seventh Report of Session 2002–3, *Trade and Development at the WTO: Issues for Cancun*, p. 7 (citing Oxfam's written submission to the Committee's inquiry).
22 This is what the Trade Justice Movement means by 'trade justice': not free trade, but trade rules weighted in favour of poor people and the environment.
23 United Nations Development Programme (1997) *Human Development Report*, p. 82.
24 Rodrik, D. (2001) *The Global Governance of Trade As If Development Really Mattered*, New York: United Nations Development Programme.
25 World Bank (2002) *Global Economic Prospects*, Washington DC, p. 168.
26 Rodrik, D. (2001) *The Global Governance of Trade As If Development Really Mattered*, New York: United Nations Development Programme, p. 22.
27 Ha-Joon Chang (2002) *Kicking Away the Ladder*, London: Anthem Press.
28 Meles Zenawi, Prime Minister of the Federal Republic of Ethiopia, oral evidence to the UK Parliament's International Development Committee. Cited in the House of Commons International Development Committee's Seventh Report of Session 2002–3, *Trade and Development at the WTO: Issues for Cancun*, p. 16.
29 United Nations Development Programme (2003) *Making Global Trade Work for People*, London: Earthscan.
30 Rodrik, D. (2001) *The Global Governance of Trade As If Development Really Mattered*, United Nations Development Programme, p. 27.
31 House of Commons International Development Committee, Sixth Report of Session 2003–4, *Migration and Development: How to Make Migration Work for Poverty Reduction*.
32 Diagram from House of Commons International Development Committee, Seventh Report of Session 2002–3, *Trade and Development at the WTO: Issues for Cancun*, p. 26.
33 World Trade Organisation (2001) *Doha Ministerial Declaration*, paras 13 and 14.
34 Diagram from House of Commons International Development Committee, Seventh Report of Session 2002–3, *Trade and Development at the WTO: Issues for Cancun*, p. 29.
35 Rodrik, D. (2001) *The Global Governance of Trade As If Development Really Mattered*, United Nations Development Programme, p. 7.

36 House of Commons International Development Committee, First Report of Session 2003–4, *Trade and Development at the WTO: Learning the Lessons of Cancun to Revive a Genuine Development Round*.
37 The G20 is a grouping of many of the largest developing countries including China, India, Brazil and South Africa, with a focus on reducing the developed world's agricultural production subsidies and eliminating export subsidies. The G90 is a grouping of the poorest developing countries, including existing preference holders. The G33's members are focused on maintaining the ability to protect their own agricultural sectors.
38 Patricia Hewitt, 'We Will Act for the World's Poor', *Guardian*, 23 June 2003, p. 16.
39 UNCTAD's 2004 Report on the Least-Developed Countries, *Linking International Trade with Poverty Reduction*, refers to three pillars which are needed to make international trade a more effective mechanism of poverty reduction. One is improving the international trade regime, including the WTO. The other two are better national development strategies, and improved international assistance for developing production and trade capacities.
40 Sheila Page, 'Making Doha a Better Deal for Poor Countries', *Financial Times*, 27 July 2004, p. 17. On compensating developing countries that lose out from liberalisation, see also Sheila Page and Peter Kleen, 'Special and Differential Treatment of Developing Countries in the World Trade Organization', paper for the Ministry of Foreign Affairs, Sweden, August 2004.
41 The Integrated Framework for Trade-related Technical Assistance to the Least Developed Countries is a multi-agency, multi-donor programme that assists the LDCs to expand their participation in the global economy, in order to enhance their economic growth and contribute to their poverty reduction strategies.
42 Overseas Development Institute and Christian Aid (2003) *A Review of the Trade and Poverty Content in PRSPs and Loan-related Documents*.

Chapter 11

43 Anderson, S. and J. Cavanagh (2000) *The Top 200: the Rise in Global Power*, New York: Institute for Policy Studies.
44 J. Bendell (2003) 'Corporate Accountability and International Regulation of TNCs', presentation summarised in *Conference News – Corporate Social*

Responsibility and Development: Towards a New Agenda? Report of the United Nations Research Institute for Social Development (UNRISD) Conference, 17–18 November 2003, Geneva.
45 UK Environmental Regulation, CBI, July 2004.
46 Stephen Timms, UK Government Minister for Corporate Social Responsibility, in speech to the World Wildlife Fund (WWF) fringe meeting at the 2002 Labour Party Conference.
47 A recent job advert for a CSR post at Virgin Group specified that knowledge and experience of marketing and PR were 'essential'. In contrast, knowledge of social and environmental issues was not even mentioned (advert issued March 2004).
48 UNRISD (2004) *Corporate Social Responsibility and Business Regulation*, Research and Policy Brief 1, www.unrisd.org
49 Friends of the Earth International (2001) *Towards Binding Corporate Accountability*, briefing paper, available at www.foei.org
50 World Summit on Sustainable Development (2002) *Plan of Implementation*, available at www.johannesburgsummit.org Para. 45ter.
51 The Green 8 consists of: Birdlife International, The Climate Action Network Europe, European Environment Bureau, Friends of the Earth Europe, Friends of Nature, Greenpeace European Unit, Transport and Environment, WWF European Policy Office.
52 The Corporate Responsibility Coalition (CORE) is a broad grouping of over 100 UK-based environment, human rights and development organisations, think tanks and trade unions, including Action Aid, Amicus, Amnesty International (UK), Catholic Agency for Overseas Development (CAFOD), Christian Aid, Friends of the Earth, Save the Children, New Economics Foundation (NEF), T&G Union, Traidcraft, Unison and Unity Trust Bank.

Chapter 13

53 Castles, S. and M. Miller (2003) *The Age of Migration*, Basingstoke: Macmillan, third edition.
54 This figure, however, does exclude irregular migrants, whose numbers are impossible to estimate accurately. IOM (2003) *World Migration Report*, Geneva: UN/IOM.
55 Adepoju, A. (2000) 'Issues and Recent Trends in International Migration in sub-Saharan Africa', *International Social Science Journal*, 52 (165): 383–94.

56 The dumping of the EU's agricultural surpluses on developing economies has devastated domestic, rural livelihoods, generating rural–urban migration. Greater competition for jobs in urban areas in turn creates additional migration pressures.
57 Joppke, C. (1998) 'Why Liberal States Accept Unwanted Immigration', *World Politics*, 50 (2): 266–93.
58 Measures include fines on airlines carrying undocumented passengers, security fencing at borders, and the wide use of visa requirements.
59 Ageing populations in the developed world indicate that demand for foreign labour will continue to rise.
60 Cornelius, W. A., Martin, P. L. and J. F. Hollifield (eds.) (1994) *Controlling Immigration: a Global Perspective*, Stanford: Stanford University Press.
61 Freeman, G. P. (1995) 'Modes of Immigration Politics in the Liberal Democratic States', *International Migration Review*, 29 (4): 881–902.
62 Sassen, S. (1996) *Transnational Economies and National Migration Policies*, Amsterdam: Institute for Migration and Ethnic Studies.
63 Collyer, M. (2003) 'Explaining Change in Established Migration Systems: the Movement of Algerians to France and the UK', Sussex Migration Working Paper No. 16, Sussex Centre for Migration Research, University of Sussex, March; King, R., Mai, N. and M. Dalipaj, M. (2003) *Exploding the Migration Myths*, London: Fabian Society and Oxfam.
64 Nyberg Sørensen, N., Van Hear, N. and P. Engberg-Pedersen (2002) 'The Migration–Development Nexus: Evidence and Policy Options', CDR Working Paper 02.6, Copenhagen: Centre for Development Research, March.

Index

accountability 36, 65-6, 69-70, 94, 105, 111, 114-24, 143
Africa 19, 23, 27-8, 30-2, 40, 44, 69, 81, 84-6, 89, 96, 104, 126, 141; Central 23; North 36-7; sub-Saharan 30-2, 35-7, 40, 81, 84-5, 126; West 23, 89
African, Caribbean and Pacific (ACP) countries 25, 96
Agreement on Textiles and Clothing (ATC) 25
agriculture 20, 22-8, 82-4, 88-91, 95-9, 131, 142; bananas 25-6, 115, 117; beef 90; cotton 23, 89; dairy 24; dumping 23, 89, 91; groundnuts 27-8; rice 26-7, 90; standards 97; sugar 23-4, 82-3, 89, 90, 95-6
aid 4, 8, 19, 26-7, 35, 39, 46, 49-50, 59, 81, 86, 97, 99, 130-1, 138; food aid 26-7; overseas development assistance (ODA) 35, 39, 49, 131; *see also* global levy
Algiers Charter 10, 12
Allende, Salvador 108
Amnesty International 75
Arab states 32
Argentina 24
Asia 27, 30, 32, 36, 81, 85, 104; Central 36; East 32, 36, 81, 104; South 32, 36-7, 81, 85; South East 30
Association of South East Asian Nations (ASEAN) 17, 51
Australasia 30
Australia 30, 96
Azores 25

Balkans 76
Bangladesh 27
Barbados 95
Barber Plan (1971) 12
Benin 23
Blair, Tony 14
Brady Plan 40
brain drain 127, 131
Brandt Report 12, 54
Brazil 23-4, 96, 137
Bretton Woods conference 10, 43, 52-3
Burkina Faso 23, 31
Burundi 31
Bush, George W. 29

California Public Employees' Retirement System 112
Canada 25, 30, 67
Canary Islands 25
Cancun Summit (WTO, 2003) 29, 85,

90, 93-4, 96
capital flows 11-12, 35-45, 53-4, 131
capitalism 7
Caribbean 25, 30, 36, 95-6
Central America 25, 104
centralisation/decentralisation 68
certification schemes 111, 115
Chad 23
Chile 78, 108
China 18, 27, 30, 67, 86, 103-4, 111
Citigroup 112
citizenship 65-6, 71, 119, 144-5
civil society 50, 70
civil rights movement 136
Cold War 9, 74-5
Colombia 23
Common Agricultural Policy (CAP) 22-4
communism 9, 13
comparative advantage 82, 84, 95, 103
Compensatory Financing Facility (CFF) 42
Confederation of British Industries (CBI) 116
Conference on International Economic Cooperation 12
consumerism/consumer action 5, 67, 82-4, 105, 111, 114-17, 143
Contingency Credit Line (CCL) 41-2
corporate accountability 114-24
Corporate Responsibility Coalition (CORE) 122-3
corporate social responsibility (CSR) 4, 108, 111-12, 114-16, 118, 121, 123
corruption 48, 75, 86
Country Coordinating Mechanisms (CCMs) 47
credit 40-2, 60-1
Crete 25
Cripps, Stafford 10

currency devaluation 11-12, 17, 21, 53-5

de Gaulle, President 10
debt 4, 19, 40-1, 48, 52-4, 56, 60-1, 69, 97, 136, 138; debt relief campaign 136, 138
Declaration on Fundamental Principles and Rights at Work 106
democracy, and efficiency 94; and global government 65-72, 142; and international finance 43, 54; and just world 3-5, 14; and liberalisation 61; and locality 93; and multilateralism 68-71; parliamentary 75; participatory 65, 67, 93-4; and peace 76; and pluralism 75-6, 78; representative 65, 71-2; and regime change 74; and the state 65-6, 68, 71, 75-6; and trade 87, 93-4, 99; in the WTO 106; *see also* social democracy 6-9
development, export-based 59; financing 35-45; international cooperation 61; local 59; migration and 127, 130-1, 144; Millennium Development Goals 35, 38, 45, 49, 98; sustainable 93, 106, 117, 131; and trade 81-99, 142-3; WTO and 81, 85
Doha Agreement/Summit (WTO, 2001) 19, 81, 88, 90, 92, 106
Dominican Republic 24

economic growth 4, 7, 9-10, 12, 14, 30, 38, 40, 42, 44-5, 54, 58, 82-3, 85-7, 93, 98
Ecuador 26
education 3, 7-8, 30, 48-9, 68, 129-31, 137
employment/unemployment 8-9, 11,

89, 103-13, 117, 125-31
ENRON 111
environment 16, 22, 56, 66, 68-70, 95, 99, 108, 111-12, 114-24, 143-5
environmental impact assessments (EIAs) 118, 143-4
Ethiopia 86
Europe, 6-10, 13-14, 30, 36, 44, 52, 110, 113, 128, 143; Eastern 13, 30; Northern 95; Western 6-9, 13-14, 30, 83, 135-6
European Commission 94, 121
European Economic Community (EEC) 12
European Union (EU) 4, 17, 19-20, 22-6, 39, 44, 51, 69, 74, 76, 78, 83-5, 89-91, 95-6, 98, 108, 112-13, 115, 117, 121-2, 142
exchange rates 11, 17, 46, 52-5, 58
Export Credit Agencies (ECAs) 40-1
export-processing zones (EPZs) 104

Fabian Society 94
fascism 52
financial speculation 13
foreign exchange 24, 53-5, 57, 125, 131
Forest Stewardship Council 115
Framework Convention on Tobacco Control 118
France 18, 25, 90, 112
Friedman, Milton 12
Friends of the Earth 114; Friends of the Earth International (FOEI)118-20

Gambia 28
gay liberation movement 136
Gea (global economic account) 57
gender issues 99, 136
General Agreement on Tariffs and Trade (GATT) 17, 22, 26, 29, 83-4, 96, 107; Uruguay Round 22, 26, 84, 96
Geneva 19
Geneva Conventions 73
genocide 73, 76-8
Germany 9, 112, West 9
Global Central Bank 57
Global Clearing Fund 55, 56-7
Global Commission on Migration 130
global commons 57, 119, 144; Global Commons Council 57
Global Environment and Trade Organisation (GETO) 54-5, 56
Global Fund to Fight AIDS, TB and Malaria 47, 51
global issues networks (GINs) 50
global justice movement 4-5, 135-40
global levy 4, 46-52, 141
Global People's Assembly 58, 69-72
global public policy networks (GPPNs) 50
Global Reporting Initiative (GRI) 112
Global Resource Pool 55-6
Global Resources Index 56
Global Social Trust Network 48
global union federations (GUFs) 105, 110, 112, 143
globalisation, anti-globalisation campaigns 138; and civil society 50; and democracy 54, 68, 142; and employment 103-13; and human rights 73-8, 105; institutions of global governance 16, 18, 21, 28-30, 56-9, 68-71, 73-4, 78, 92, 96-7, 105, 107, 142; and just world 3-5, 14; and labour 104-7, 139; and migration 125, 128-9; and monetary regulation 4, 10-11, 35-46, 54, 58, 68; and neoliberalism 46; and policy space 92-3, 142;

progressive 46, 74, 83, 98; and redistribution 46-7; regressive 74; and regulation 105; social democracy and 7-8, 14, 73, 141; social dimension of 107; and social policy 46-7; and the state 5, 73-4, 78; and taxation 46-7, 51; and trade 83
gold standard 10, 52
grassroots 4-5
Greece 23, 25
Green 8 group 121
green movement 115-16
gross domestic product (GDP) 27, 45, 46, 84
Group of Eight (G8) 17-18, 39, 50, 107
Group of Ninety (G90) 93
Group of Seven (G7) 50
Group of Seventy-seven (G77) 120
Group of Thirty-three (G33) 93
Group of Twenty (G20) 51, 93
Guadeloupe 25
Guatemala 23

Haiti 86
Haliburton 112
Havana Charter 104
Hayek, Friedrich von 12
health 7-8, 19, 47-9, 55, 69, 84, 109, 117, 119, 127, 130
heavily indebted poor countries (HIPCs) 40-1, 43
Hewitt, Patricia 94
HIV/AIDS 84
Honduras 26
housing 7-8, 68, 127, 129, 131, 139
Human Development Index (HDI) 30-1
human rights 4, 16, 69, 73-8, 105-7, 114-15, 119-20, 123, 142-4
Human Rights Watch 75

IBM 66
IFC 41
India 24, 27, 30, 66, 103
Indonesia 27
industry 24-5, 56, 92, 111
inequality 7-8, 30, 69, 126, 130
infant mortality 31
inflation 11-13, 58
institutions, credit 40; economic 35; of global governance 16, 18, 21, 28-30, 56-9, 68-71, 73-4, 78, 92, 96-7, 105, 107, 142; and the global justice movement 4; local 93; and the market 3; and poverty 3; and trade 10
Integrated Framework 97
interest rates 9, 11-12, 14, 40, 56-7
intergovernmental organisations (IGOs) 69-71, 142
International Clearing Union 10, 52-5, 58-9, 141
International Confederation of Free Trade Unions (ICFTU) 112
International Convention on Corporate Accountability and Liability 120
International Criminal Court 77, 119, 142
International Criminal Tribunal for former Yugoslavia (ICTY) 77
International Finance Facility (IFF) 35, 38-9, 45, 141
international financial institutions (IFIs) 36, 43-5, 141
International Labour Organisation (ILO) 48, 51, 56, 104-9; Declaration on Fundamental Principles and Rights at Work 106; Tripartite Declaration of Principles Concerning Multinational Enterprises and Social Policy 108; . World Commission on the Social

INDEX

Dimension of Globalisation 107
International Monetary Fund (IMF) 13, 17-18, 25, 38, 40-5, 53-4, 57, 69-70, 86, 96, 99, 107, 126, 139, 141-2
International Organisation for Migration 129
International Right to Know Campaign 118
International Trade Organisation 104
Internet 13
investment 7, 9-14, 21, 35, 40, 45, 53-5, 57, 82, 85, 92, 98, 103-6, 108-9, 111-12, 115, 121, 130-1, 141, 143
Iraq 28-9

Jamaica 24, 89, 95
Japan 25-7, 30
Johannesburg Earth Summit *see* World Summit on Sustainable Development

Kant, Immanuel 78
Keynes, John Maynard 10, 12, 52 4
Kosovo 29

Labour Party (UK) 14
labour, child 106; and collective bargaining 104, 110; and corporate accountability 117, 119-20; exploitation of 7, 106-7, 129-30; flexibility of 12, 129, 139-40; global market in 21; globalisation and 104-7, 139; and health and safety 109, 117; and human rights 105-7, 143; and migration 125-31, 144; mobility 88; movement 135-8, 140; plant closures and 109; prison 106-7; protection of 4, 129-30, 139; regulation of 7, 143; and relocation 103; rights 56; and social democracy 135; standards 104, 107, 111-13, 119; wages 56, 104, 139; *see also* trade unions
Latin America 30, 32, 36, 69, 81, 137
Left, progressive 4-5
less developed countries (LDCs) 19, 21, 84, 89, 91
life expectancy 30-1, 67, 69
literacy 30
Lomé Convention 12, 25

Madeira 25
Malawi 23, 28
Mali 23, 31, 86
Martinique 25
Mauritius 86
McDermott 112
McDonald's 67
Mercosur 17, 51
Mexico 26, 40, 85
Microsoft 66
Middle East 11, 36-7
migration 99, 125-31, 144
militarism/military regimes 75-8, 83, 142
Mill, James 65
Millennium Development Goals 35, 38, 45, 49, 98
Milosevic, Slobodan 78
Monterrey Consensus 35-6, 39, 43, 45
Multifibre Arrangements (MFA) 25
Multilateral Agreement on Investment 108
Multilateral Development Banks 40
multinational companies 11, 13, 105, 107-10, 113, 114, 118, 125, 129, 139-40, 143-5
Myanmar 27

National Contact Points (NCPs) 109-10

National Social Trust Organisations 48
natural resources availability 58-9,
　119, 144
neoliberalism 4-5, 12-13, 28, 116,
　137-8, 140, 141
Nepal 86
Netherlands 30
networking 48, 50-1, 136-40
New International Economic Order 12
Niger 31
Nigeria 28
Nixon, Richard 10-12
non-governmental organisations
　(NGOs) 47, 51, 70-1, 74, 108-11,
　116-17, 121-2, 142
North Atlantic Treaty Organisation
　(NATO) 17, 29
North/South 4-5, 12, 21, 28, 88-91,
　98, 103-4, 120, 137-40
Norway 30
Nuremberg Trials 73

oil 11, 57
Organisation for Economic
　Cooperation and Development
　(OECD) 17-18, 24, 31, 48, 104,
　108-10; OECD Guidelines on
　Multinational Enterprises 108-10
Organisation of Petroleum Exporting
　Countries (OPEC) 11, 17
Oxfam 20

Pacific region 32, 36, 96
Paine, Tom 78
peace 16, 18, 69, 73-8
Peru 86
Philippines 27
Pinochet, Augusto 78
pluralism 75-6
policy space 92-3, 142
Portugal 25

poverty 3, 7-8, 22-4, 36, 39, 42, 45,
　46, 48, 53, 70, 81-99, 126-7, 130-
　1, 142
Poverty Reduction and Growth
　Facilities (PRGFs), 40, 42
Poverty Reduction Strategy Papers
　(PRSPs) 43, 48, 97
Prebisch Report 10
protectionism 7, 9-10, 19, 21-30, 81,
　85-6, 90, 92, 97, 104

al-Qaida 78

racism 127, 129
Reagan, Ronald 108
refugees 16, 126
regionalism 5, 142-3
regulation 3-4, 7, 13-14, 35-45, 46,
　56, 68-9, 92-3, 103-13, 114, 116,
　120-1, 143
Right, New 4-5, 7
Rio Principles 120
Rio Tinto 112
Russia 18, 29
Rwanda 74, 77

Saddam Hussein 78
Scandinavia 7
Seattle Summit (WTO, 1999) 29, 93,
　137
Second World War 52, 73, 104, 128
Senegal 27-8
September 11 catastrophe 74, 78, 127
Serbia 74, 78
service sector 5, 103
Sierra Leone 31
Singapore Issues 85, 93-4
social democracy 6-10, 13-14, 73-4,
　78, 135, 140, 141
social justice 9, 11, 73-4, 110, 114,
　117, 123

social movements 71, 135-40
social welfare 3, 7-9, 11, 48, 70, 126, 130-1, 142
socialism, revolutionary 6; social democratic 6-10, 13, 137, 140
socially responsible investment (SRI) 114
South Africa 24, 28
South America 25
South Asian Association for Regional Co-operation (SAARC) 51
South Korea 86
Southern African Development Community (SADC) 51
Soviet Union 9
Spain 23, 25
special and differential treatment (SDT) 92
Special Drawing Right (SDR) 55
state, and capital flows 11; and capitalism 7; and democracy 65-6, 68, 71, 75-6; and globalisation 5, 73-4; and GPPNs 51; and human rights 75; and immigration 128; and inflation 11; intervention by 7, 27; and investment 7, 9-12; and multilateralism 69-71; ownership by 7; and poverty 42; and progressive change 4-5; and regulation 104, 108, 117; social democracy and 10; and trade 58, 83
structural adjustment 42, 45, 126
Stuttgart 107
subsidies 9, 20-4, 26-7, 42, 55-6, 81, 84, 89-91, 95, 99, 109, 119
sustainability rate 56-7
Sweden 30

Taiwan 86
taxation 7, 9, 13, 46-7, 51, 55, 83-4, 121
technology 56, 83-4, 103, 131
terrorism 74-8, 138; 'war on terrorism' 77
Thailand 24, 27
Thatcher, Margaret 108
Tobin Tax 46
Togo 23
trade, balance of 52-9, 141; chaos 52; conflict 53; and democracy 87, 93-4, 99; and development 81-99, 142-3; discriminatory 22-8; fair 115; free 9, 13, 21-2, 28, 52, 82, 85-6; equitable/inequitable 81-99, 130, 142; global negotiation of 4, 17, 22, 83; and instability 11; and institutions 10; international currency and 9-12; and just world 3, 14; and labour 106-7; liberalisation of 20, 27-8, 30, 81-99, 106, 126, 138, 143; and poverty 81-99; preferential trade agreements 19; quotas 24-7, 91; sanctions 20-1, 26, 39; and the state 83; tariffs 21, 23-7, 55-6, 83, 90-1, 95-7; terms of 36, 42; *see also* protectionism, World Trade Organisation (WTO)
trade-related intellectual property rights (TRIPs) 84
Trade Union Advisory Committee of the Organisation of Economic Co-operation and Development (TUAC) 112
trade unions 4, 7, 13-14, 46, 103-13, 114, 122, 143; global union federations (GUFs) 105, 110, 112, 143
transaction fees 57
transparency 36, 48, 58, 70, 94, 106, 118, 121
Trinidad 95
Tripartite Declaration of Principles Concerning Multinational

Enterprises and Social Policy 108
'truth and reconciliation' processes 77

United Kingdom 9, 14, 18, 29, 35, 38-9, 45, 52-3, 86, 93-4, 97-9, 112, 114-17, 122-3, 140, 141
United Nations (UN) 12, 16, 18, 21, 39, 51, 56-7, 69, 73-8, 96, 99, 105, 108, 142-3; Code of Conduct for Transnational Corporations 108; Convention on the Rights of Migrant Workers and their Families 130; Covenant on Economic, Cultural and Social Rights 49, 69; Economic and Social Committee (ECOSOC) 51; General Assembly 16, 18, 69; Genocide Convention (1948) 73; Millennium Project 40, 49; Secretariat 16; Security Council 16, 18, 29, 51, 73, 77; Universal Declaration on Human Rights (1948) 73
United Nations Commission on Sustainable Development (CSD) 56
United Nations Conference on Trade and Development (UNCTAD) 56, 96
United Nations Development Programme (UNDP) 49, 56, 84, 96
United Nations Educational, Social and Cultural Organisation (UNESCO) 51
United Nations Research Institute for Social Development (UNRISD) 117

United States of America (USA) 8-10, 12, 16, 18-20, 23-30, 44, 52-3, 67, 69, 74, 76, 84, 86, 89-91, 98, 108, 112, 120, 136; Farm Act (2002) 23, 27
Unocal 112

Venezuela 137
Vietnam 27, 86
violence 77
Volcker Plan (1972) 12

White, Harry Dexter 52-3
women's movement 136
Works Council Directive 113
World Bank 13, 17-18, 21, 25, 44-5, 47-8, 50-1, 53, 56, 69, 85-6, 99, 107, 126, 139, 141
World Commission on the Social Dimension of Globalisation 107
World Development Movement (WDM) 19
World Health Organisation (WHO) 51
World Summit on Sustainable Development (Johannesburg, 2002) 118-20
World Trade Organisation (WTO) 17-20, 25-9, 56, 69-70, 81-99, 104-7, 126, 139, 142
World Water Contract 49

Yugoslavia 77

Zambia 23, 86, 140